YOU'RE
TOO GOOD
TO FEEL
THIS BAD

An Orthodox Approach to
Living an Unorthodox Life

NATE DALLAS

Copyright © 2020 Nate Dallas

ISBN: 978-0-578-64342-7

Contents

Introduction

YOU PROBABLY PICKED up this book because the title resonated with you. You're too good to feel this bad, and you know it. You've likely been thinking it for years, unsure of what to do with that sentiment. And now, you're here, book in hand, with a uniquely tailored opportunity. This book started as a collection of personal handwritten notes. They were the ideas, insights, questions, and answers I came across in my dedicated pursuit of a better life. I originally compiled these notes for myself, but apparently, I wrote them for you too.

A few years back, I kicked off an intense search for ways to ease the stress harassing my mind and the physical ailments plaguing my body. And I discovered a trove of awesome stuff. Rich insights and powerful practices were hidden in some ordinary places and also in some strange ones. My self-experiments went a little extreme because that's the only way I knew how to do things. I've chronicled the ones that worked best in this book, and I've even highlighted a few that flopped. My hope is that these words will both entertain and inspire you.

Personal growth is always a multi-faceted process, which means the trek inevitably becomes complicated and overwhelming. To prevent mental overload and analysis paralysis, I arranged this guide in a practical and achievable sequence. We'll gather small wins early and use that initial momentum to achieve more substantial victories later. I've also

1

compartmentalized the big-ticket items so you can tackle them one at a time. The pieces will eventually all fit back together into a consummate mosaic portrait of your best self.

The beginning steps are mostly physiological, revisiting the fundamental areas of life we too often neglect. As we progress, we'll add more psychological and intellectual elements. Our work will shift from straightforward actions to deeply contemplative ones. We'll stroll into powerful insights on satisfying basic human needs, breaking preexisting patterns, and bolstering an elite mindset. That progression will feed directly into practical strategies regarding work, play, and relationships. By the end, you will be a more calculated, more fulfilled, healthier, and stronger person.

I encourage you to spend adequate time in each chapter and practice the methods within until becoming proficient. Resist the urge to fly through the material. This is not a race, and consciousness should come before habits. Some may need to spend weeks, if not months, on a given chapter. Allow time to ponder, understand, and implement the concepts. We create lasting change by taking control of the things that control our behaviors. We modify inputs to improve outputs.

If you picked this up because a single chapter interests you, welcome. Reading and applying even just one section will benefit those willing to practice. Harness your passion and curiosity for that topic and attack it with a precision focus. Just know that there are many other elements contained in other chapters that will supplement your chosen interest. All these chapters work synergistically to construct a more dynamic impact than if addressed alone.

Bottom line: this stuff works. Small decisions do influence dramatic transformations. And whether you willfully take on a single chapter or systematically work through all of them, you will see results. These pages are full of opportunities to grab onto something that resonates with you. When that happens, run with it! No one else can do the work for you. No matter your approach, I want to challenge you to set three expectations before embarking on this thrilling journey:

First: Expect results. Choose to be optimistic about the impending benefits. They are many.

Second: Expect that this process will require discipline, perhaps more than you believe you currently possess. That will build as we go.

Third: Expect to tackle this work alone. Be willing to be a solo contrarian, even if no one else understands what you are doing.

There are undoubtedly many ways to experience a breakthrough and to awaken your best self. I won't pretend that this book is the absolute solution for everyone. Still, I do adamantly believe there is something for everyone here. As I implemented the life-altering methods in this book, I began to experience a transformational shift in emotional peace and physical well-being. Those results are available to you too, and I will show you exactly what I did to make it happen. Sometimes we don't need another lecture as much as we need better tools. I am delighted to present you with a specialized and robust toolbox to use as you see fit.

Finally, be patient. Sustained growth requires persistence and repetition. Please take your time and enjoy the process, even when it's demanding. These elements will cascade into something beautiful and powerful if you allow them.

Peace be with you on your journey.

And I agree with you: you're too good to feel this bad.

CHAPTER 1
Waking Up

THE POTENT DRUGS were wearing off. I knew where I was and why, but I was very disoriented. I could barely hold my head up, and I didn't want to talk too much because I knew I still sounded wasted. But my mind was processing, hyper-focused on the details around me: the light piercing through the blinds, the condensation on the water pitcher, the stitching on the sheets, and the soft knock on the door. The doctor entered the recovery room to give my wife the report. I suspected what he would say; the diagnosis would confirm his prior intuition, validating his thirty years of specialist experience. It would also permanently alter my life.

The twelve months leading up to that pivotal day were tough. Discomfort, confusion, and fear, all symptoms that had been present for several years, had strengthened in both frequency and intensity. New ailments were manifesting without warning. I knew something was seriously wrong, but I couldn't believe that after all my hard work and discipline that I could still be this sick. I was too good to feel this bad. Most people had no idea that I was physically suffering because I just powered through it, business as usual. I would see 40 patients each day at my dental practice, run multiple side businesses during lunch break and on my commute, and return home to my wife and children to eat dinner as a family and tell bedtime stories. My wife was the only person who knew how bad my condition had become. She also knew I had no plans to pull back.

Slowing down wasn't a viable option. My businesses, commitments, and family were robust and still growing. They would likely be even bigger next year. None of these things could reasonably run without me. No other person could carry out all of my roles, not even temporarily. No one else on the planet knew how many accounts, investments, businesses, products, charities, and ongoing projects I had in place. So many people depended on me. This reality was not a surprise, just a natural byproduct of what I had built. I wasn't complaining about it. I knew that it was all part of the deal.

During that year, I had seen multiple doctors for scans, tests, screenings, adjustments, lab work, treatments, and medicines. Regardless of who I consulted, they all had a similar message, and it went something like: "You are one of the healthiest people that comes into this clinic. We don't see anything noteworthy in your tests. This medicine may help your symptoms. Give it a try. Good luck." No one knew quite what to do with all of my unrelated symptoms or how to help. I never felt like they were even listening. As much as I hated to admit it, I needed to see a specialist.

After months of patiently waiting for an appointment, I had my first consult with the "gut guru," Dr. Y. We hit it off. He laughed at my jokes as he listened to various parts of my body with his cold, shiny stethoscope. Then after asking a series of questions, he dictated all of my symptoms into the computer:

"Patient complains of nightly insomnia: often with waking night terrors and vivid hallucinations. Daily headaches. Occasional debilitating migraines, often with vomiting. Daily stomach pain for several years:

increasing frequency. Diarrhea: three to five times per week. History of asthma. Excessive list of food allergies: multiple allergy tests confirm the list is increasing and intensifying. Frequent neck and shoulder pain: requires regular chiropractic adjustment and electrostimulation, constantly maintained back pain, poor memory. The patient exhibits clinical findings of audible, heavy, stomach fluid movement. Pain to pressure in the anterior abdomen and kidney areas."

Whoa. It was jarring to hear them all lumped together like that. My mind was racing, clipping through an all too familiar list of harrowing possibilities. There had to be an explanation, and I knew it had to be something serious. I honestly couldn't decide if I wanted to know what it was. I had researched various cancers, tumors, and debilitating diseases, wondering which one afflicted me. Dr. Y told me we needed to proceed with a colonoscopy, more labs, and likely a few biopsies of inflamed areas inside my GI tract. I told him that I was in for whatever we needed to do, at any cost. I sat up in my chair and mustered up the courage to ask my burning question. My voice cracked as my mouth suddenly became desert dry. "So, what do you think this is?"

Dr. Y turned and situated himself directly in front of me. His change in position and direct eye contact demanded my attention. He knew something, and I was about to know it too. He told me he didn't want to get ahead of the next appointment, but that he had seen cases like mine before. I listened intently, optimistic, but terrified.

The good doctor went on. "I think the problem is that you are very stressed." I sat there dumbfounded, simultaneously realizing how quiet that clinic was and how loud my mouth breathing had become. I was just about to ask, "Is that all you've got?" when he reiterated his former statement. "I think all of your symptoms are due to stress and anxiety." A brief, awkward pause followed, indicating that it was my turn to speak.

"Stress and anxiety?" I muttered as if to say, "You're joking, right?" After all, stress was the vague answer that lazy doctors gave when they couldn't come up with a precise one. I respectfully disagreed and informed him that I didn't feel stressed and anxious. "I love my life. I'm not unhappy. I'm grateful for where I am and what I have. I feel like I am in my prime." Dr. Y interrupted my spiel to inform me that our definitions of stress were different. He said, "Your body is clearly functioning as if it is under extreme stress." He continued to explain that my system was always in fight-or-flight mode, even though I wasn't emotionally miserable. He said it was "not uncommon for highly productive people," which didn't make me feel any better.

Dr. Y projected his opinion in a more convincing way. "Your brain is always active, even when you are trying to sleep. It never rests, does it? People like you just cannot shut it off." He said that he had several patients like me and that some people are just "wired that way." He told me that my body was ill because it was exhausted, that I needed to rest both my body and my mind. He informed me that we would proceed in a few weeks with the colonoscopy but reiterated that he thought the problem was a simple, one-word diagnosis.

All I could think was, "Freaking great! Now what?" I pondered my rebuttal, considering whether he could be right. After all, I was born this way: a dreamer, a doer, a creative, and probably a little A.D.D. too. But those things are not handicaps; they're my superpowers. I naturally have extra energy and require little sleep. An aversion to laziness is in my DNA. These assets are part of my temperament and fit well with what I am trying to do. After what must have been a significant period of silence, Dr. Y said, "OK, so we'll do the colonoscopy next and go from there. Good visit."

He let me know that a few prescriptions would be waiting for me at the pharmacy. Sarcastically, I replied, "For what? A vacation and a personal assistant?" He explained that one medicine was an anti-spasmodic to get my stomach to stop churning, and the other was an anti-anxiety medication. I emphatically responded that I was not a "medicine guy," especially when it came to mind-altering drugs that could change my state, energy, and engagement. I told him that I didn't want the anxiety stuff, reminding him that I had to function at a high level. Being sedated all day or, worse, becoming dependent on mind-altering drugs was not an option for me. He pushed me to accept a half dose, only at bedtime, for just 30 days. He said it would help me sleep and assured me that I would feel normal each morning after. I reluctantly agreed, planning to figure this stuff out before ever finishing the bottle.

With a smirk, the doc asked, "You don't watch TV, do you?" I told him I gave that up many years ago. He recommended that I "give myself permission" to watch some standup comedy videos once in a while in the evenings. I asked him if my joke delivery needed some work, and he said that it would be beneficial to do something enjoyable that didn't involve learning. He added, "Your body needs a signal to know that you are finished working." I informed him that I used red wine to communicate that signal every evening.

I drove away from the consult feeling somewhat dejected but slightly relieved, too. I hoped the diagnosis was correct but had desired something more definitive. After all, stress is a wide-ranging, ambiguous foe. Could this massive smattering of longstanding symptoms and issues be a result of anxiety and stress? Seriously? If so, I had faith to know I could come up with a plan to beat it. *I'm resilient, persistent, and disciplined,* I assured myself. *Heck yeah, I can whip this! How did I slip into this mess, like a lazy person with no control? Wait a second. There is no way that it could be this simple. Surely, it's a brain tumor or colon cancer. I must at least have some pituitary problems. But what if I don't? That's fantastic!*

My mind continued to race. *Hold it! What about all the other people who are genuinely stressed? What about people who can't afford to see a specialist? What about people whose marriages are falling apart or who have just lost their jobs? What about those who are alone or have no energy? What about people trapped in a much worse place? How bad is their diarrhea? I bet they have constant headaches. There must be millions of those people. What an awful thing. How sad. Is that why so many people take sick days at work? I don't take sick days. There's too much to do.* At that moment, the woman at the pharmacy drive-through window said, somewhat aggressively, like she was repeating it for the second time, "Dr. Dallas, your scripts are ready." My stomach rumbled as a familiar abdominal cramp started. How long had I been sitting there? I didn't even remember driving to the place. How many thoughts had just sprinted through my mind? How many more were coming?

I immediately tried the spasm medicine for my churning stomach. I hadn't even pulled away from the drive-through before opening the bottle. From the window, I noticed a portly, middle-aged woman at the walk-up counter inside. I assume she was a regular. She had been watching me pop my pills as she waited for her meds. I made eye contact with her just after I swallowed the bitter tablet without any liquid. She quickly looked away, probably thinking about what a hopeless addict I must be. I signed my receipt as the pharmacist informed me that my high income/low benefit insurance coverage sucked even more than I thought. The $10,000 deductible and $2100 per month premiums didn't cover much for stress and loose stools, which only exacerbated my newly diagnosed condition.

I took the anxiety medicine that night as directed. The next morning, I felt fine as I poured my first cup of coffee. The gurgling sound of the hot beverage hitting my ceramic mug reminded me of the dream I just had. In it, I was fly fishing beside a familiar waterfall with my annual fishing buddy. This was a significant realization because I had not been able to remember a pleasant dream in years. I rarely dreamed at all. The only ones I remembered were frightening and tense, resulting in me leaping up out of bed to fight whatever dangerous situation, demon, or dreadful person had attacked during my fractured slumber. I was always forced to be a frustrated hero in my dreams, springing into action because of other people's negligence, lack of attention, and ignorance. I had already decimated two lampshades that year, mistaking them for intruders. My wife was not a big fan of my fictional roles as an action hero while quasi-sleeping.

But this day was different. It was a little more peaceful. I noticed that I didn't get nearly as impatient or frustrated with my employees or my children. Before, I had always tried to refrain from showing those emotions, but I knew they were bottled up inside me. I worried that one day the pressure would build so high that I would erupt like a geyser, finally losing it and spraying the inner contents of my mind everywhere with reckless abandon. Thankfully, my level-headed father had taught me self-control, and I managed to hold it together for another day. Score one more for the home team!

I used the medicine for a few weeks, but only when I felt mentally exhausted or overloaded. My mind was still busy all day, but I seemed to be resting better at night. I arrived early for my colonoscopy appointment after following my pre-game instructions. If you have never prepped for such a procedure, let's just say that it's eventful. Your entire GI tract must be empty, which means everything in there must be flushed out. Everything! There is a uniquely formulated beverage for accomplishing this goal with astounding efficacy. What an adventure. If I ever needed to attack an invading army, I would get mass amounts of that stuff in their water supply ASAP.

I stripped down and put on the pastel, open-back gown as instructed. A nurse rolled me down the hallway with my IV bag dripping. I had never been on the passenger side of a gurney before. The nurse pressed a button on the wall, exactly like the ones I had pushed to unlock the double doors before witnessing all five of my children being born. The next thing I remember, I was in the recovery room next to my wife, with Dr. Y sitting in front of us.

It was time for the report. What did the doctor see on the tiny camera that traveled the treacherous path through such a despicable port of entry? What was my condition? What would it mean for my children, my career, my longevity? My wife seemed at ease. What had I missed? What had Dr. Y told her before I came to? Every time I voiced a question, my wife would lightly pat my leg, exactly like I had seen her do with her 99-year-old great aunt, Tia, when she was disoriented. I had many questions but couldn't get them out. In a foggy stupor, I asked Dr. Y three different times if I had hemorrhoids, but that was not what I was trying to ask. I wanted to know if he found a tumor, an ulcer, or a parasitic alien life form. He mostly spoke to my wife. He only occasionally spoke to me as if I were a toddler who just woke up at 3:30 in the morning, asking about his missing dragon. I heard her say, "So everything was totally fine?" I lost the audio, but Dr. Y gave an affirmative nod as he mouthed something positive to her. He made tornadic motions over his head, followed by side-to-side hand movements in front of his stomach with a sour face.

The next time I woke up, we were entering our neighborhood. I was emotional, but in a good way. I was grateful to know that I wasn't dying. I told my wife I felt fine and planned to mow the grass and jump on the trampoline with the kids. A few hours later, I awoke again in my bedroom. There was no noise in the house, which was remarkable. I walked into the kitchen to find a beautiful woman preparing a plate of food.

She had quarantined all the kids to the yard. She hugged me, then pulled out my chair and said, "Dr. Y said you did great. Everything is fine. He said it's just stress because you are such a machine." With firm resolve, I promised her I would figure it this stuff out and get better. "I know you will," she said and pushed my plate toward me.

That night, I ordered three new books on gut health, neurology, and psychology. I also ordered the first of many test kits to start measuring vitamins, minerals, essential elements, hormones, markers, enzymes, heavy metals, toxins, yeast, bacteria, metabolites, antioxidants, and anything else I could to obtain useful data. It was time to take a deep dive into what was happening inside my body and determine what sustainable solutions were out there for remedies. I planned to test as many methods as possible until I found a few that worked. I had no idea that I would eventually test dozens, if not hundreds, of products and practices over the next two years. I didn't want to base my results merely on how I felt. I wanted accurate, tangible data. For the next few months, the family became accustomed to regularly finding urine sample containers next to the veggies in the freezer. Blood, saliva, and hair samples became commonplace as well. It was time for me to figure it all out and beat this thing.

A New Dawn

In the early stages of my recovery, I naively thought my condition was unique, ignorant of the fact that many of the successful people around me were in similar situations. Evidently, people don't talk about these things too openly. I don't know if it's that we are embarrassed or just too busy to take the time to share. Maybe it's a simple lack of community and connection. Regardless, I took the road alone, without a guide or mentor. I didn't know anyone who was in the same boat, much less someone who had successfully made it out of the storm. So, I just planned to do the only thing I truly knew how to do: Launch, then learn on the fly and make adjustments as I went.

What ensued was a whirlwind journey of recovery, rebuilding, and rebirth. If you had told me how dramatically things would improve, I would have been a skeptic. I'm conscious that I have an addictive personality, so I wasn't surprised when the three books turned into several dozen more. The reading compounded with hundreds of hours of training courses, podcasts, and educational videos. I was hungry for improvement and expected to find some. What I did not expect was that I'd totally redesign my life, one element at a time. Progress became my drug of choice, and it was in abundant supply.

I was clueless about the possibilities that were available, accessible, and free to all of us. I assumed that a modest 5% to 10% improvement in overall health, wellness, and happiness was possible. Going three days without a pounding headache or speed-walking to the bathroom would have been amazing. Small adjustments started having big impacts as each element seemed to build on the next with exponential and synergistic effects.

The ongoing lab results mirrored what I was feeling in real-time. My high cortisol (stress hormone) level dropped, as my low serotonin and dopamine (happy hormones) levels rose. I started getting high on life. My brain chemistry changed, and so did everything else. The numerous deficiencies noted in my prior reports began disappearing. My relationships improved. Over time, my mind became sharper, more attuned, and less distracted. I learned how to be less triggered, more fulfilled, and to experience true peace. I learned how to rest, in body, mind, and spirit. The way I saw the world and my role in it shifted. The way I connected with people elevated. My sense of fulfillment and satisfaction improved, and the fear and feeling of entrapment I'd been wrestling with diminished.

I realize retrospectively that many overachievers have a false sense of security when it comes to health and happiness. I certainly did. We inaccurately believe that life is good enough, or at least as good as it can reasonably get. We make excuses for our lousy condition and justify staying there. The real problem is that our standards are too low, and our vision is lacking. We're not broken; we're just a little too "normal." We are stuck in the middle but fail to realize it because we are doing noticeably better than most.

The problem is that we genuinely have no idea of what lies outside of the mediocrity. We don't even question the possibilities because we are ignorant of them. Our measuring scale is inadequate. We compare our lives to those of sick people, not to the people that are thriving. I was one of the healthiest and happiest people I knew, but only because I measured myself within the median range of sick, unhappy, stressed, depressed, angry, broke, bored, unfulfilled folks. I am now functioning as an anomaly, several standard deviations away from the mean. I thought only monks and mystics could exist in this realm.

Why This Book? Why now?

I started helping a few people (they call it "coaching" now) after vetting these powerful practices myself. I never intended to; it happened organically. I don't know why they decided to come to me instead of someone else or how they found me, but they did. Many of them already had doctors, therapists, pastors, counselors, or coaches. Before I knew it, friends, family, and even strangers were coming out of the woodwork. Without warning, people would get comfortable and unload on me. It was uncanny. They would share things that they had never

You're Too Good to Feel This Bad

shared with anyone. There was some positive change cooking in the kitchen, and once people smelled it, they became hungry.

Once I started sharing the insights and strategies now contained in this book, other people started changing too. People were working out their rocky marriage, returning to lead their families, getting off antidepressants, eliminating longstanding debt, receiving promotions at work, losing weight, feeling stronger and more energetic, developing courage, dating again, loving and being loved, becoming more charitable, simplifying, finding peace, and building an entirely different future.

Every person I was able to share the feast with wanted to bring more people to the banquet. I love the one-on-one approach, but there is only one of me. Even with massive amounts of new margin appearing on my schedule from simplifying life, I could not service all the requests for help. But I also believed it would be selfish not to share. Suddenly, writing this book felt necessary.

But here's the disclaimer: this book isn't for everyone.

I am not such a dreamer as to think that this material is for every person who picks it up. It's not. This manual is for proven doers. It's for those people who sincerely hunger for growth and don't require extra external motivation every day to do demanding work. Most people have goals, but the majority don't attain those goals. What most people do get is their standards. The three-word, simple takeaway from this book may be: *raise your standards*. Better standards require us to remove some things and add some others. They force us to accept some things and refuse to accept others. At this point in life, you don't need another lecture. You probably only need a few new tools, and perhaps a quick demo.

Beyond desire and hunger, this book is for people who have already been through a few of the natural stages for highly productive people. Failures come first, likely many times.

16

Success hopefully arrives next, and then comes the stuff in this book. I say this because people who have not been through the first two stages, failure and success, will not be ready. Success doesn't teach us much, but it does give us confidence that we can do it again. Failure, suffering, and setbacks are typically the place where we experience the most learning and growth. Without a certain amount of resilience, humility, discipline, and honesty, this stuff can't work. Those traits prepare fertile ground for new growth, so when seeds blow by, they have a chance to sprout.

The Plan

All of these methods will require practice and repetition. The elements that have the most value and impact will require the most effort. However, the dividends from the investment will keep paying out for years to come. You will live a more abundant life. The awesome thing I am discovering about this process is that living a healthier, more fulfilled, more peaceful, and more playful life actually takes less work than living the way I was living before. It is a rare opportunity in life to be offered an upgrade for a lower price. Don't pass it up! The overused phrase, "Work smarter, not harder," certainly applies.

I began experiencing this material as a curious novice on a meandering path. You don't have to be as lost as I was, although I am grateful for the process as I experienced it. I have developed a sequence for you based on well-vetted practices and verified results. There's no way that you can implement this stuff and not improve. No way!

You will experience events, people, and processes in a more vibrant, more connected way. You will have the tools that you need to change any situation, any mood, and any outcome. You will look differently, speak differently, and see differently. You will be less angry, triggered, and envious. You will be more confident, grounded, and consistent. You will have a clearer path and a sharper focus. People will gravitate toward you as you genuinely enjoy life more. You will experience more order and freedom. Your human connections will deepen. You will understand why you do what you do, and in turn, why other people do what they do. You will be able to remove wasteful objects, tasks, and people from your life. You will change the way you work and your relationship with money. You will rediscover what it feels like to be a child at heart.

My promise to you is that I will not waste your time. I know it is valuable. We will move quickly and intentionally. I am grateful that we are both here now, and your attention honors me. I'm pumped, knowing that you are about to climb onto the rocketship and launch to a new place. Trust the process. Follow the script. This ride has the real potential to change everything.

IN REVIEWING MY overstuffed journal to write this book, I now have a better understanding of a point explained by Carl Jung. He said that the greatest and most important problems of life are all, in some sense, insoluble. They cannot be solved, but only outgrown. E.F. Schumacher said it a bit differently, but he parallels Jung by saying, "Divergent problems cannot be killed… They can, however, be transcended." This is only the case, "where self-awareness plays its proper role." Thanks to good fortune, or what the religious call grace, I do feel like many of my problems were gifts. They are opportunities and continue to be. As strange as it may sound, I think the verb *transcended* more accurately describes this process. Whether outgrown or transcended, my problems were not solved as much as they were left behind during a period of maturation. About halfway through this manuscript, when you hit your stride, there will be an opportunity for your deeper, more genuine self to awaken too. This part of you has always been there, and it is good. Now might be the time to stretch it out and let it breathe. I sincerely hope so, because you are too good to feel this bad.

CHAPTER 2
Lying in Plain Sight – Sleep

I F THERE IS a single goal in this book that we should be militant about mastering, it's achieving high-quality sleep. I'll show you a simple system to do that in this chapter. Before you spend another dime on products promising to improve your health and productivity, get this stuff going. No superfood, vitamin, or drug on the planet can accomplish what good sleep achieves. Proper sleeping will:

- Make you live longer and look more attractive
- Increase your memory, focus, and mental cognition
- Protect you from cancer, dementia, and the common cold
- Make you feel happier and enhance your sex life
- Lower your anxiety, decrease your depression, and improve your relationships
- Speed recovery times and prevent injuries
- Make you more creative and a better problem solver

Anyone with a decent head on their shoulders knows they should make sleep a priority. But how many of us actually do it? So many other elements in life seem to take higher precedence, stealing the attention that sleep deserves.

There was a time in my not so distant past that I would

brag about not needing much sleep. Like so many other foolish entrepreneurs and high-energy creatives, I thought I was a unique breed that could operate on little sleep with no consequences. Looking back on it now, it would be like me bragging that I could still do my work while intoxicated. As far as brain activity goes, that's precisely what I was doing: functioning with only a fraction of my capacity. *Look at my neat circus trick! I can stumble around in a foggy stupor and still file taxes for three corporations on time. For tomorrow's show, you can watch me forget what my wife asked me to do as I locate my misplaced keys!* Sleeping five or six hours a night didn't make me a hero; it only reinforced what an idiot I was for enduring needless suffering. The fact that I ignored such fundamental knowledge and kept sleep on the back burner for as long as I did still perplexes me—and thinking about what those choices might've cost me is infuriating.

According to the Centers for Disease Control and Prevention, 30% of adults in the US and Canada are sleep deprived. And that number includes a large population of older, retired adults who get plenty of rest. Your demographic likely represents a more staggering number. The World Health Organization classified sleep deprivation as an epidemic, and we have every reason to assume that the impact is serious.

We cannot do peak work, whether physical or mental, without sufficient sleep. Proper sleep regulates hormones that control energy, focus, appetite, attitude, happiness, and sex drive. Without it, we cannot function optimally. Poor sleep also compromises our immune system. We are three to five times more likely to get a cold or infection when sleep deprived. Even a flu shot is 50% less effective if the recipient is poorly rested.

Being awake too long causes damage to the brain. More awake time means more damage, and sleep is our only opportunity for necessary repair. After being awake for 19 hours straight, we are as impaired cognitively as someone legally drunk. After only four hours of sleep, a driver is six times more likely to run his car off the road than someone who had eight hours of rest. But it's not just one exceptional late night that compromises us. Going a week and a half straight on seven hours of sleep per night produces the same test results as 24 hours with zero sleep. You don't even want to know the results of the studies that look at five hours of sleep plus alcohol, which is a nightly combo for many people today.

Make no mistake: poor sleep always negatively affects the mind, body, and spirit. There is no escaping this truth, so if you are serious about living, you must be serious about sleeping. Until you get on the right track with sleep and take a retrospective look back, it's impossible even to fathom how tremendously things will improve. And for that reason, garnering a solid understanding of this chapter will be worth more than any other activity you could be doing right now.

What's Your Magic Number?

I'm not sure how much sleep I was getting before my liberation, but it was nowhere near the recommended eight hours per night. Even if I had tried to get eight hours, there would have been no way to pull it off. My brain was too busy. I would have stared at the ceiling for two hours before falling asleep if I went to bed "early." I wasn't sleepy. Well, at least not at the opportune times when normal people should sleep. I was tired while playing board games with my kids, or better still, when driving down the interstate or while performing a root canal. Like a little brat, I didn't want to sleep when I was supposed to. I despised having to stop moving. Now, I would hand over my bank account and all my hobbies before I would surrender my sleep again.

I noticed some textbook benefits once I found a solid sleep groove.

- Heightened mental acuity and focus
- Boosted libido
- Increased strength and endurance
- Elevated mood and self-control
- Reduced allergies, ailments, and illnesses
- Improved patience
- Enhanced memory

Eight hours is the recommended goal for adults, but that's not a rigid number, and it doesn't apply to everyone. Some people require a little less or a little more. But before you jump on the "I don't need much sleep" train, hear me when I say you probably do need more than you think. You probably also need way more than you have been getting. Your number will have to be tested and tweaked over time. The goal of eight hours is the standard starting point.

Here are a few questions that might assist in determining if you are getting enough sleep:

- If the power went out and your alarm clock never sounded in the morning, would you sleep past your wake-up time?
- Do you hit the snooze button before getting out of bed?
- Are you groggy in the morning upon waking, taking a while to ramp up to a functional level?
- Do you require a second or third cup of coffee during the day to keep going strong?
- Do you forget parts of your day, like driving?
- Do you struggle to finish your workout?
- Do you know what day it is right now?
- Do you stay irritated with chipper people and fantasize about knocking them out?

- Do you repeatedly come close to burning your house down, requiring you to rent ozone machines to get rid of the horrible smoke smell because you forgot the food on the stove again?

OK. The last two might only apply to me. But, if the answer to any of these was "yes," you likely need more rest or, at minimum, better quality rest. I have solutions for both.

What is "Good" Sleep?

It's not just the number of hours asleep that matters. The quality of your rest is also of major importance. Adequate, healthy sleep involves a fascinating, repeating cycle involving REM (rapid eye movement) sleep and non-REM sleep. When we fall asleep, we enter the non-REM stage first, which causes our heart rate to slow, and our body temperature to drop. As we get further into the non-REM stage, we enter deep sleep, where the body repairs and grows tissues and strengthens our immune system. After a deep non-REM stage, we move into a REM stage, which is the dream state. In this stage, our brain becomes more active and processes all the information from the day, storing what we have learned into memory. The full cycle through non-REM and REM sleep lasts about 90 minutes. Once complete, the cycle continually repeats for the duration of our slumber.

Two main factors determine when we sleep and how deeply we do so:

1. Circadian rhythm
2. Adenosine accumulation

Let's take a deeper dive into both.

Circadian Rhythm

Our bodies prefer to get into a regular sleep cycle and a daily routine. Thousands of years of human evolution have given us an incredible internal clock that matches very closely to a day. The human biological clock is not precisely 24 hours, but it's darn close. And that internal clock changes our body's temperature at different times of the day, adjusts our metabolic rate based on the current rhythm, and produces energy for when we should need it. In short, our circadian rhythm determines when our brain ramps up and when it shuts down, and it provides us with supplemental functions to have better wakefulness and better sleep. If we allow our bodies a consistent cycle, the results are undeniable. When we get out of sync and change the routine from one day to the next, we confuse our system, and the strategically precise times get bumped around, causing a cascade of damaging events.

One study showed a 24% increase in heart attacks in the springtime when we lose an hour of sleep due to the time change. In contrast, there is about a 21% decrease in heart attacks in the fall when we gain an extra hour of sleep. (Sandhu et al., 2014) It's one reason why daylight savings time probably needs to be eliminated.

The key to utilizing circadian rhythm effectively is *consistency*. We need to keep a steady schedule for sleep and waking, but that's easier said than done when living in a crowded household or a city that never sleeps. On top of that, most people won't do what they need to do to master their circadian rhythm. Few of us are willing to change our schedules, adopt new discipline, and train our bodies properly. As I said in the opening chapter, this book is not for everybody. But for those willing to shake things up a bit and make some bold moves, your efforts will not go unrewarded.

Adenosine Accumulation

The second factor that determines when we sleep is chemical. Adenosine is an important neurotransmitter that binds to receptors in our brain, inhibiting our nervous system and making us sleepy enough to get the rest that we need. It's a byproduct of the breakdown of adenosine triphosphate (ATP) molecules, which store and transmit the energy needed for our cells. Adenosine levels continually rise every hour that we are awake. As adenosine builds in our system, more and more of it binds to the receptors in our brain, inhibiting arousal and making us sleepier. As adenosine accumulates, the urge to sleep intensifies. At peak adenosine levels, we must sleep to prevent serious damage. Then, as we sleep, adenosine levels drop. The rate of adenosine metabolism and clearance determines how long we sleep as well as the quality of that sleep. For an average adult, it takes about 8 hours of sleep to clear 16 hours of adenosine buildup.

So, if you've been paying attention, you now know why we're using 8 full hours of sleep as our target. After 16 hours of wake time, it's time to go to sleep, and after 8 hours of sleep, it's time to wake up. More than 16 hours of adenosine accumulation forces your performance to quickly and exponentially degrade; less than 8 hours of recovery is insufficient for adequately clearing it from your system. Without sufficient clearance, we cannot process and file away the things we learned the previous day or store them into our memory. So, while adenosine and circadian rhythm are independent of each other, the results are potent and beneficial when both are in sync. And when they are not, many of our bodily processes get confused, and we suffer for it.

Other Key Players in the Sleep Game
Melatonin

Now that there is a basic framework in place, it's an opportune time to introduce a new character in the sleep drama. Meet melatonin, a naturally occurring hormone that tells your brain when to sleep. Think of it as a reverse alarm clock letting your body know when it's time to end the day instead of when to start. Melatonin does not affect how deeply you sleep, but it greatly influences how sleepy you become each day.

Melatonin gets released into your body mostly after dusk. When light dissipates, and your brain perceives darkness, the hormone level increases. In a natural setting without flashing billboards and overhead kitchen lights, melatonin activity initiates at sunset. It continues for a few hours until it reaches a peak that cues you to go to sleep. Like adenosine, as melatonin builds in the system, we become sleepier.

But here's where it gets tricky. Any light source, whether natural or manmade, will delay and reduce melatonin release. The problem in modern-day society is that we have lights everywhere. They shine at all hours of the day and night. This includes the numbers on the alarm clock, buttons on the wireless router, streetlights, and screens that stay in front of us for way too many hours of the day. When exposed to too many lights for too long, we miss out on the sleepy benefits of melatonin—and some lights are bigger offenders than others. All lights affect our sleepiness by blocking melatonin, but certain wavelengths of lighting, like the blue spectrum lights found in many LED fixtures, are worse. Those energy-efficient, LED lights can block 50% more melatonin than other sources.

Without a calculated plan to combat lights in the evening, we are victims of our own technological advances. We shouldn't surrender so much of our precious melatonin to artificial light and screens. Choose to mimic nature as best you can by reducing as many lights as possible when the sun goes down. If you are mindful of your light exposure and protective of your melatonin, you will see many opportunities to reduce light exposure and reap the benefits.

Common Killers

Unfortunately, light isn't the only culprit stealing away our high-quality sleep. Brace yourself, because some of your other favorite things might be on this hit list.

Caffeine

Caffeine has become ubiquitous in modern society. People use it and abuse it all day and all night. Oddly enough, there is no public scrutiny for this addiction or even any standards to designate what is socially acceptable. Never mind that caffeine is likely *more* addictive than some other frowned-upon vices because of the harmful vehicles we use to deliver it, such as the sugar-loaded sodas and artificially flavored energy drinks lining the drink aisle at the store. So many people drink hot milkshakes masquerading as coffee as a daily practice. That 500-calorie, mocha-frocha-choca-woppa-latte is not doing any favors for your brain or your muffin-top. Stop drinking daily desserts. That much sugar should only be consumed once per year anyway. It's called your birthday.

But we love what caffeine does for us, don't we? After all, it reduces sleepiness, allowing us to work more hours and feel more energized. But few of us understand what happens after the mug hits our lips. Caffeine does not produce energy, as often advertised. It merely delays sleepiness by blocking adenosine. Caffeine binds to the very same receptors in the brain that are needed to bind adenosine. When caffeine attaches to the receptors, adenosine gets blocked from binding to the site. Remember, adenosine accumulates every hour we are awake.

Therefore, when caffeine is on board, we don't get as sleepy as we should because the adenosine is left in the system with nowhere to express its sleep signals.

The half-life of caffeine is around six hours. This term defines the point at which half of a substance is no longer biologically active, but that doesn't mean it's out of your system. At the twelve-hour mark, up to 25% of the caffeine we ingest can still be active. That means the americano you drink at 10:00 a.m. could still be significantly blocking adenosine at 10:00 p.m. When the caffeine is finally metabolized and wears off, the binding sites become available again, and adenosine rushes in to attach. This is what we experience with a caffeine crash, and the longer we consume caffeine and stay awake, the bigger the pending crash will be.

We cannot escape daily levels of rising adenosine. At some point, it must be cleared with sleep.

Beer, Wine, and Spirits

Alcohol is the next bombshell on the list. Many of you don't want to hear it, and I didn't either. I had a glass (or more) every night for over a decade. It was part of my decompression routine. I was convinced that it helped me go to sleep, and it served as an essential cap to end a long day.

The truth is that alcohol is a sedative, which means it will *sedate* you, not make you sleep. Sedation (unconsciousness) and sleep are not the same things. Drinking alcohol may make you a better dancer and make you feel sleepier after the party, but you won't stay asleep or sleep deeply. Alcohol breaks the natural sleep cycle and disturbs healthy sleep. It also blocks REM sleep, which is another reason why some people can't remember much after a binger. But it's not only the night of the bad karaoke and cheesy pick-up lines that is compromised. A single night of drinking can cause sleep disturbances for several nights. The takeaway message here is simple, albeit inconvenient for some and downright painful for others: alcohol is terrible for your sleep. If you are going to be serious about your health and your slumber, you cannot ignore these facts.

Sleep Aids

Sleeping pills are widely used and likely over-prescribed today because of so many people's preventable, poor sleep habits. The problem with most of these pills is that, much like alcohol, they fail to produce quality sleep. Several prescription drugs taken for insomnia, such as Ambien®, are classified as sedative-hypnotics. These medicines sedate us by shutting down areas of our brain, but they do not produce natural sleep cycles. They also come with a host of possible side effects, including memory loss.

Many people take over-the-counter products to help with sleep. Some of these will make you groggy beforehand but can turn you into a nocturnal maniac a few hours later. Short-term supplementation of melatonin might be occasionally helpful to reset your clock after jetlag, but none of these sleep aids should stay in place over extended timeframes for healthy people. They can negatively alter your natural production of sleep hormones over time. We need a long-term, sustainable, healthier option. That option will become available by forming better habits.

Essential Sleep Strategies

You now have a basic understanding of adenosine, melatonin, and circadian rhythm. Building on your newfound respect for caffeine and alcohol, let's lay out a system of practical habits to achieve superior sleep. Here is the official You're Too Good to Feel This Bad Top 10 List.

Strategy #1 - Maintain Rhythm

Lock in a concrete bedtime and wake time that allows for a full 8 hours of sleep. (Fine-tuning and recalibration can occur later. For now, a full eight hours is the starting point.) Religiously adhere to both times for at least two weeks to establish a consistent circadian rhythm. Clear your schedule to make it possible or wait to initiate the practice when you have a feasible calendar without late-night events or travel. If an occasional late night makes you miss your target bedtime, still adhere to the set wake time and go to sleep earlier the next night if you need to do so. Try not to disturb your waking rhythm by sleeping late, either. A consistent wake time is critically important for good rhythm, even on the weekends. Grab a nap later in the day if you need one. If a siesta is required, snag one at least three hours after your set wake time, and at least four hours before your bedtime. A fifteen to thirty-minute nap is great for a recharge. However, unless you are sick or elderly, daily naps should not be required once you start sleeping well at night.

Stay consistent, even when it sucks. When I started my sleep odyssey, I selected a 10 p.m. bedtime and a 6 a.m. wake time. I'm not going to lie. Those first few days were terrible. I wasn't sleepy at 10:00 because my routine was so sporadic. Yet, regardless of whether I finally fell asleep at 10:40 or 12:15, I still faithfully arose when my alarm bellowed at 6:00 each morning. I fought the urge to get a few Z's during my lunch break, hoping to be exhausted by 10:00 when I hit my pillow. After a few days of struggle, my system began to adjust, and after two weeks, I was in the groove. Our bodies adjust to the new routine and provide maximum resources based on the regular schedule. When your work schedule and meals are consistent too, your body will begin to provide peak energy during those times of higher demand.

Strategy #2 – Turn Down the Lights

Most modern smartphones and tablets have a night setting, which reduces the blue light automatically. Find this setting and change it over if available. At a minimum, reduce the brightness on all screens to the lowest levels, starting at dusk each day. Wear regular sunglasses daily in the late afternoon whenever you are outside. An additional option is to wear special glasses inside after dark. Many manufacturers now make blue-blocking glasses for indoor use. If you want to try these, wear them after dark at home, especially when using your laptop, phone, tablet, or when watching TV. You can make fun of me for looking like Bono wearing my yellow lenses in the evening, but not when you look like Beetlejuice in the morning.

Regulate your home lighting and turn off all unnecessary lights after dark. Use strictly non-blue lights for the last few hours of the day. Turning off half of the house lights makes a measurable difference. I switch from bright overhead lights to smaller wattage, non-blue lamps after sunset. Blackout as much of the bedroom as possible by placing dark coverings over windows. Block electronic devices that emit light. Change your bedside lamp to a lower voltage, dimmer, non-LED light bulb. Installing dimmer switches on light fixtures is beneficial too. I changed a few of my switches myself after watching a few how-to videos online. If you don't know your way around the hardware store, aren't very handy, or just have a healthy fear of high voltage or death by electrocution, hire a professional.

Strategy #3 - Keep Your cool

Temperature is just as powerful as light when it comes to sleep. Our core body temperature must drop three to five degrees each night to sleep well. We sleep better if we are a little chilly rather than a little warm. It's easier to fall asleep in a cooler atmosphere, and we achieve deeper sleep there, so drop your home thermostat a few degrees two hours before bedtime and bump it down another few when you head to the bedroom for the night. If you have a programmable thermostat, set it to drop through the night gradually. Wear less clothing and use less bedding so that your body temperature can drop more efficiently. I wear socks when I sleep because my feet get cold and keep me awake. The rest of my body prefers the lower temperature and rewards me for it. Socks also substantially improve my ability to moonwalk.

Strategy #4 – Stick to the Ultimate Duo for Bedroom Basics

Our brains tend to associate behaviors with different settings and stimuli. With that in mind, reserve your bed for two purposes: sleep and sex. That's it. Don't eat or watch TV in your bed. Don't check your email, browse social media, or crochet. If you do read in the late evening, stick to peaceful, pleasure reading only. No horror thrillers! And no working! If your phone is too much of a temptation, leave it in the other room or in a drawer, and don't forget to switch on the "Do Not Disturb" mode. In my home, I have a set chair for meditation, a separate spot for reading, and a reserved sanctuary for sleep. If I want to be entertained, I do it elsewhere. When I want to sleep, I go to my bed. Train your mind to associate your bed with sleep and only sleep. In time, after compounding these strategies, your body will be conditioned to fall asleep quickly after crawling into your sheets.

Evening sex stays on the list because it promotes better sleep in numerous ways. For starters, physical exhaustion demands sleep. Most people also do the deed in the dark, so our melatonin isn't threatened. Beyond that, there are some chemical and hormonal benefits. The body releases prolactin after orgasm. Prolactin is a powerful hormone, typically more abundant in men. It suppresses dopamine, which is the neurotransmitter that stimulates us and makes us feel more awake. Oxytocin, also known as the "feel-good hormone" or the "cuddle hormone," is also released during intimate activity. It helps to vanquish stressful thoughts from your mind, making it easier to relax afterward. When you combine oxytocin, prolactin, melatonin, and a side of lactic acid from muscle fatigue, you have a pretty potent sleep cocktail. You may both be delighted to find that when you start sleeping like a sane human, playful romps before your morning coffee become a preferred option as well.

Strategy #5 - Cut the Caffeine

If coffee or tea is a part of your daily routine and you want it to remain so, drink a cup (or two) upon waking and be done with it for the remainder of the day. In time, as you layer the strategies in this book, you won't need the extra caffeine to make it through the day. Eventually, you will despise afternoon caffeine because you will notice how it affects your sacred sleep routine. And while we're at it, just stop drinking sugar altogether. This will avoid two types of crashes. That means no caramel lattes, sodas, or energy drinks.

Strategy #6 - Anchor the Alcohol

Alcohol should be reserved for special occasions. Special occasions are not to be classified as such if they happen more than once or twice per week. A work night or a Netflix binge by yourself, for the third time in a week, is not a special occasion. If you get invited to a special event, only RSVP "yes" to those happening on the weekend, preferably around midday. OK, that last one is a bit tongue-in-cheek, but I recommend that you try what I did: Give up all alcohol for 30 days. I'll be honest and admit that it was tough for a while. Although I wasn't abusing alcohol or getting out of control, I was addicted to my nightcap. Drinking was also a standard component of the social activity that I crave. You might feel the same, but I encourage you to try it anyway. To my delight and surprise, refraining from imbibing didn't bother anyone at the functions I attended. Just know that any time you are going to give up something pleasurable, it probably needs to be replaced with something great. Go for some dark chocolate, a tasty smoothie, or something else that feels like a treat. My body is much happier and stronger without regular alcohol, and I have yet to meet anyone who doesn't agree that a consumption reduction was super beneficial.

Strategy #7 – Establish Regular Rituals

Besides just having a prescribed time to go to bed and to rise, it's profoundly beneficial to have other consistent routines around those times. These things function as cues to signal to our brain what's coming next and allow our bodies to adjust to provide resources at the right times. When we eat, work, read, exercise, recreate, meditate, all matter. Try to do these things at the same time each day, so your body can learn the patterns. Eat meals at consistent times and refrain from eating large meals close to bedtime. If your routine doesn't allow for three or four regular meals on a steady schedule, try eating small portions regularly every few hours to keep your metabolism going. Setting your workouts at a consistent time each day helps establish a better circadian rhythm as well. Just try not to do heavy exercise within three hours of bedtime. My body responds favorably to a cold shower in the morning and a warm one in the evening. In fact, a warm shower before bed actually helps to lower body temperature.

Strategy #8 - Limit Your Screen Time

The last hour before bedtime should be screen-free. Most mobile devices now have a setting for automatic shutoff using "screen time" or "do not disturb" settings. Lock yourself out of your own devices on a sensible schedule. Silencing and disabling all sounds and notifications produces significant benefits too. If your device is too much of a temptation, leave it in another room and use something else for your morning alarm. Watching TV or scrolling social media until you feel tired is a mistake. The added light and extra stimulation are not doing your sleep any favors. Neither is the current media trend that intentionally stirs up anger to keep audiences engaged. In general, a riotous urge to punch people in the face or set buildings on fire does not contribute to harmonious slumber. I also stopped checking emails at night because it required a screen and initiated many new thought processes that I didn't want spinning in my head.

Strategy #9 - Set a Bedtime Alarm

A pre-set, consistent time to rise each day is essential. The next step is to set alarms or notifications for bedtime and pre-bedtime. The pre-bedtime announcement should be about an hour before bedtime. The first phase is when we start dialing everything down: activity, lights, temperature, screens, and so forth. Stretching, followed by a warm shower is a great start to a bedtime routine, as well. Relaxation breathing is a favorite next step for many. Others listen to light music, read, meditate, color, or work crossword puzzles until they reach the second alarm. This final time goal is when the lights officially go out, and your head hits the pillow. You can develop and refine the pattern that works best for you.

Strategy #10 - Don't Get Worked Up. Get Worked Down

Occasionally we lie in bed, awake, not tired enough to fall asleep. This mild insomnia may especially be the case when you're in the beginning phases of establishing proper rhythms. Don't fret or get frustrated. If it takes more than 15 minutes to fall asleep, and you still feel wide awake, get up. Resume your quiet, mild, pre-bedtime activities until you get sleepy. Avoid screens and keep physical activity low, but do something other than lie there, anxious, thinking about how badly you wish you were asleep. I like to read, journal, or plan the following day in these gaps. A few times per month, for a host of complex reasons, our rhythm may be a little off. Manage it calmly and go back to bed once you feel a strong urge to sleep. If you have a bedtime audible like some of these I have described, still maintain your standard wake time the next day.

The final note to close this chapter out concerns sleep-tracking devices. I am a big fan of testing and data, since everything you measure tends to improve, and highly recommend tracking your sleep. My personal favorite is the Oura ring, but there are many products available today to track sleep patterns: mats for your bed, bedside table units, and wearable monitors like bracelets, rings, and headbands. If you have some extra cash and you want to check the data, grab a device, and try it for a few weeks. It won't directly help you sleep but may help encourage you to practice the ten steps above by validating your progress or highlighting daily mistakes.

The bottom line is that if you want to perform at a high level with less stress and anxiety, you must get serious about sleep. All other efforts and methods will be restricted without this one in place. These strategies work, and I encourage you to start practicing all of them as soon as possible. How about tonight? Start incorporating these sleep strategies into your life and make them a top priority. Your mind, body, spirit, spouse, family, friends, boss, coworkers, clients, and pets will all be glad you did. Get some rest. You probably need it.

CHAPTER 3
Get with the Flow - Breathing

THE MOMENT WE are born, our bodies automatically execute the most essential function for immediate survival. We breathe. Tragically, that initial inhale is one of the few times in life many of us do it correctly.

Our muscles expand and contract in rhythm to keep air flowing 24 hours a day for 30,000 days or so. We breathe more than we do anything else, and therein lies an unfortunate reality: most of us never learn how to do it well. Improper breathing creates unnecessary suffering and a lower ceiling for human potential; it caps how well we can perform and forces us to get by on limited oxygen, reduced blood flow, and diminished brainpower. Most of us get by well enough to stay alive and function—but we shouldn't accept life in the mediocre middle, should we?

Every organ in our bodies needs oxygen, and every one of them suffers if it does not receive an adequate supply. Concentration, focus, mental cognition, sleep, energy, endurance, immunity, recovery, and digestion all depend on oxygen. Breathing is also a profound way to cope with stress. It affects our blood flow, heart rate, and even our hormone signaling. It also affects our pH (the body's acidity level), which influences almost every human process. Breathing may even influence body pH more than what we eat and drink!

Today is a perfect day to learn the ways of the breath. Let's get into it.

The Basics of the Breath

We won't get too bogged down in biology and chemistry, but it is essential to review a few things from your high school science classes. If you are like me, you weren't paying attention back then. You probably remember more about the doodles in your notebook than the lesson on the dry erase board... or was it chalk? Hopefully, you can absorb and apply the information now that you aren't dodging spitballs from across the room.

When we breathe, we inhale oxygen (O_2) and exhale carbon dioxide (CO_2). *You do remember that part, right?* Incoming oxygen enters the lungs and then passes into the bloodstream. Our blood is full of red blood cells (RBCs), and those RBCs grab the newly available oxygen molecules and carry them throughout the body to deliver them to tissues in need. RBCs are also the transport vehicles for returning the CO_2 to the lungs to be exhaled back out. They carry both oxygen and carbon dioxide efficiently because they are full of specific proteins called hemoglobin. We must have a sufficient RBC and hemoglobin count to exchange and move these gases. A simple blood test can confirm that your RBC and hemoglobin counts are healthy.

When we take in air, it travels into our lungs. To quickly refresh you on lung anatomy, there are two of them, one on each side of our upper body. They are sacs, narrower at the top, where air enters and exits, and broader at the bottom. Inside the bag is a system of bronchi, bronchioles, and alveoli. The structure is much like an inverted tree, starting at a trunk and separating into limbs, which eventually divide into smaller branches. At the tips of each branch, there are lots of tiny balloons called alveoli. These little sacs are where the oxygen and carbon dioxide exchange happen. Oxygen enters the blood through these alveoli. Carbon dioxide also gets removed from the blood through the same sites. With an image of lung anatomy imprinted into your mind, the first rule becomes apparent.

Breathing Rule #1 – The Most Efficient Air Exchange Takes Place in the Lower Lungs.

The reason for this rule is twofold:

1. There is more room for air in the lower, broader areas of the lungs.
2. There are disproportionally more alveoli in the lower sections of the lungs to do the vital work of exchanging gases.

If we manage to get air into the lower, more substantial portion of the lungs, there is an opportunity for more oxygenation with less effort and waste. This concept is simple enough and probably not groundbreaking. However, without fail, whenever I'm doing a speaking gig and ask a crowd of people to take a deep breath, I see the same sight every time. In cartoon-like fashion, as if they are the wolf about to blow down a swine house, I watch a room full of chests rising and expanding. This widespread practice of full-chested breathing is wrong. It may be a big breath, but that's not the same thing as a deep or effective one. A large, chest breath mainly uses the upper lungs, where we have the weakest return on our oxygen saturation and exchange rate.

Stop right now and put one hand on your chest and another on your abdomen. Take a deep breath. Which hand moves? If the hand over your chest moves the most, it's time to make some adjustments. To fill the lungs and take deeper breaths, we must work the diaphragm, the muscle that extends across the lower thoracic cavity, not the chest.

Practice this for a bit while you read: Inhale and exhale, with your belly doing the moving instead of your chest and shoulders. Keep it quiet but full. Notice how, when you use your diaphragm, the stomach stretches forward during the inhalation, which is the opposite of how most adults breathe.

Many environmental, habitual, and nutritional factors influence us to breathe poorly. But perhaps a driving reason we transition to bad breathing is simple vanity. Most men want their chests to look more prominent and their gut to look smaller. Most women want their breasts to be perky and their tummies to be tight. Don't worry, I won't suggest that you go around with your stomach poking out all day, or for you to give up your superhero pose. (And I grant you full permission to momentarily do it wrong for the sake of a beach photo.) Have no fear; proper breathing becomes invisible once you master it. Remember, there are more alveoli down there doing the work, which means you won't need to move as much air if you push it to the bottom. Breathing well means more return on less volume, thus requiring smaller breaths.

I wanted to learn to breathe using my diaphragm, but old habits are hard to break. I knew I would forget to breathe correctly in the absence of electro-shock therapy or constant reminders, so I opted for the latter. Knowing how distracted and busy I get during a typical day, I decided to set reminders and establish triggers to remind me to practice better breathing. I placed sticky notes in key places all over my home and offices. I put them in my coffee mug cabinet, on my toothbrush, laptop, and the table beside my meditation chair—all places where I would see the notes every day, thanks to longstanding habits.

(Note: Habit stacking is a useful tool in many facets of life.

Adding an additional process on top of an already rigid habit is a solid method for getting a new one going.)

The sticky notes prompted me to breathe using my diaphragm. I also set periodic notifications and alarms on my phone to remind me throughout the day. I also drew a traffic light on my notes. The sketch served as a visual trigger for my mind to associate breathing and stoplights. Soon enough, every time I saw a traffic light, I would be reminded to breathe well. If everyone adopted this practice, road rage would probably decrease by 80%.

I went a step further and wore a thin Velcro strap around my mid-chest for a few weeks. If I used my chest too much, I would hear the belt separating under my shirt and be reminded to move the air lower. I don't know what people thought when they heard ripping sounds coming from my sternum. Fortunately, the noises mostly occurred in the presence of stress-inducing people that I wasn't trying to impress.

After a few months of practice, most of my breathing was taking place in the lower areas of my lungs. I felt more energized and witnessed favorable changes in my pH. My chronic back and neck pain started to subside as I became consistent. I can only assume this was because I wasn't raising my chest and shoulders to breathe anymore. Diaphragm breathing eliminated 20,000 mini muscle repetitions per day. This loosened the tight muscles in my neck, chest, shoulders, and upper back. Little did I know, I was just getting started.

Breathing Rule #2
Smaller Breaths are the Best,
and Big Breaths are a Bust

Breathing heavier does not ensure that more oxygen makes it into the bloodstream. Furthermore, it does not guarantee that more oxygen will reach your organs, muscles, and tissues. Contrary to popular belief, big breaths are a bust. When taking larger breaths, we become more tired from over-breathing and may even be reducing the amount of oxygen we receive. Close your mouth, and I'll explain.

A healthy adult breathing clean air has an oxygen saturation (SpO2) level around 95% to 99%. We can easily measure SpO2 in seconds with a pulse oximeter attached to a fingertip. This fashionable device has become a regular piece of hand jewelry for me in the last few years of experimenting. The SpO2 number expresses the percentage of hemoglobin molecules in our red blood cells that are currently carrying oxygen. Unless there is a significant underlying issue like pneumonia, sleep apnea, chronic obstructive pulmonary disease, or other illness, saturation levels rarely fall out of the normal range. Even if it dropped to 92% momentarily while swimming underwater, the number would return to 99% within seconds of resuming regular breathing.

A saturation reading of 99% means that 99% of the molecules in the blood that could be carrying oxygen are already doing so. So, at any given moment of the day, a healthy person has an adequate supply of oxygen, almost 100% of the limit that the RBCs can hold and store. For this reason, much of the oxygen we breathe in gets exhaled right back out. It's wasted. Even if there is a burst of oxygen pulled out of storage to be used by a working muscle, our blood oxygen level quickly refills to maximum capacity. The refilling rate is generally much faster than the consumption rate. That is especially true at rest, but even the case during exercise. We have an adequate supply of oxygen in the blood, ready to be used. Our bodies only need to remove it from storage in the blood and deliver it to the body parts in need. The thing that most people don't understand is that the item that determines how much oxygen gets removed and used is the other gas, CO_2. Stick with me. Science class is almost over.

Get this! The hemoglobin holding the oxygen will not release the oxygen it carries until it is in the presence of carbon dioxide. The incoming O_2 and the outgoing CO_2 molecules exchange places in the RBC. One gets off, and the other gets on. The O_2 rides the hemoglobin through the bloodstream until it reaches the body part in need. That area of the body can only de-bond the hemoglobin to receive the oxygen it is carrying if there is a CO_2 molecule to trade.

In other words: We can have an abundance of oxygen in the blood, but without adequate CO_2, the oxygen remains trapped and cannot be used by your body. CO_2 is the gatekeeper molecule that makes that oxygen delivery possible. That means we need to keep some of it around.

You can breathe easier now that the biology and chemistry lectures are over. Let's move on to the practical skills needed to become a superhuman.

We can control multiple factors when we breathe. The first two factors to discuss are rate, how many times we take a breath each minute, and volume, the size of each breath.

When we are breathing faster or heavier, already at 99% saturation, there is no benefit to the larger breaths. In this process, we are driving off more of our CO_2 supply by exhaling more often. This reduces the number of available exchange molecules needed for our high oxygen supply. So, when breathing too much, we are lowering how much oxygen our bodies can utilize. Most people today are over-breathing and giving away too much CO_2 with each exhale. We don't need to forfeit carbon dioxide unnecessarily. Breathing less often increases the amount of CO_2 in your system, and in turn, can increase the amount of oxygen delivery. More oxygen delivery to the tissues means more performance. This O_2/CO_2 paradox is why many elite athletes train at high altitudes: oxygen is more limited in that environment, so carbon dioxide levels can be higher. It's in this combination that people can train themselves to breathe less while their muscles get super-fueled and become super-strong.

Don't start huffing into a trash bag, buy a plane ticket to Mount Kilimanjaro, or take a long walk next to the coal-burning plant just yet. Too much carbon dioxide in the blood (hypercapnia) is dangerous. It manifests with a host of symptoms like drowsiness, confusion, exhaustion, headaches, irregular heartbeat, panic attacks, or passing out. During mild periods of hypercapnia, the body automatically adjusts the respiratory rate and tidal volume to regulate and balance.

There is a simple way to keep a better balance: We must breathe into the correct area of the lungs, and we've got to breathe less. Calm, quiet, deep breathing using the diaphragm is the goal. This method ensures that we get the same amount of oxygen into storage while keeping enough CO_2 around to use the oxygen when we need it.

Once I started breathing this way, my breaths per minute dropped by about 20% because each breath was so much more efficient. I didn't need as many breaths. My oxygen saturation level on the SpO_2 monitor stayed at 99%, but I was exhaling much less of my precious CO_2. It created a baseline level of relaxation that I had never known. After correcting my breathing and posture, my massage therapist asked me what in the world I was doing to alter my muscle tension so dramatically. We could both feel the improvements in my back, neck, and shoulders. Muscle tension causes emotional tension and vice versa. I now appreciate that many people who I assumed were born with a chill, easy-going personality may simply be elite breathers.

To recap rule two, sucking in more air does not force more oxygen into the bloodstream if it's already saturated. Secondly, if there is insufficient CO_2 in the system, the oxygen cannot be used by the body. Calm, deep breathing supplies sufficient O_2 while maintaining CO_2.

The final breathing rule was the hardest for me, but probably the most beneficial. It's a game-changer but took the most practice to get right.

Breathing Rule #3:
Noses are Designed for Breathing

Besides rate and volume, we also get a third choice. We pick whether to allow air to flow through the nose or the mouth. I was primarily a mouth breather my entire life. It wasn't a conscious decision, but it was the wrong choice. Extended periods of mouth breathing can cause dry mouth, dehydration, poor sleep, lower energy, lower blood circulation, more sickness, worse allergies, and even tooth decay, bad breath, and skeletal deformities. I'm convinced that I endured a lot of unnecessary suffering because of weak mouth breathing. We should breathe through our noses all day, every day. The list of advantages of nose breathing is (cough) breathtaking.

Pulling air in through the nose activates the diaphragm more than when we use the mouth. Nose breathing increases oxygen uptake 10% to 20% more than mouth breathing. That means you can take smaller breaths and don't need as many of them. So, your body gets to relax even more when using the nose. Nose breathing also increases end-tidal CO_2, which is a measure of how much carbon dioxide stays in the blood after exhalation. Remember, we want to keep a healthy supply of that.

The nose has several other vital functions too:

- It serves as a critical air filter, removing many of the common pollutants and allergens that cause us trouble.
- There is a sterilization function unique to the nose that sanitizes the air.
- The nasal passages hydrate the air as it passes through. (Mouth breathing causes measurably more dehydration.)
- The nose also plays a role in regulating air temperature by warming the incoming air.

If you are serious about health and performance, you must be intentional about making the switch from mouth to nose breathing. It's not easy, but it's worth the effort.

I had a difficult time learning to breathe through my nose. Since I had primarily used my mouth to breathe most of my life, I had poorly developed nasal passages. The phrase, "Use it or lose it," applies and was the case for my nasal airway. It always seemed narrow, blocked, and dry—hence the mouth breathing. Regardless, I was determined to learn to use my nose correctly. I knew it would take time and practice, so I did what any reasonable person seeking growth would do. I taped my mouth shut for six months.

Yes, I taped it. I did not get a feeding tube placed into my stomach or learn sign language, although I briefly considered both. I removed the tape when I was in public, needed to eat, or had to speak. But when I was reading, writing, meditating, doing yard work, or driving alone, I was taped up. Sitting at a red light with your mouth taped is sure to produce some strange looks. I looked like a hostage and confused a lot of people, but it worked for my training purposes. If you decide to try the tape, which I highly recommend, don't use tape from the hardware store unless you enjoy ripping the skin off your face. Get a roll of the specialty tape that nurses use for taping intravenous lines to your arm. Search for Transpore® tape or Micropore® tape designed for skin and get the latex-free, hypoallergenic option. There is now even a product available called LipSeal Tape, invented by a dentist, that comes precut in the shape of your lips for a better seal.

Many people tape their mouths closed while sleeping too. I tried it for a while but never became entirely comfortable with the approach. It made me annoyed and restless to have my mouth taped while trying to sleep. Be sure to check with your physician before trying it at night, as apnea and other issues may create problems. If you have an aversion to night taping as I did, you may want to try out some Breathe Right® strips or nasal dilators. I am a fan of the strips, which fit over the bridge of the nose and help to open the nasal passages. You've probably seen some athletes wear them during games. You can peel them right off in the morning, and there's no suffocation potential. Nasal dilators are small splints that fit just inside your nose and aim for the same goal of enlarging the opening.

In time, when using the diaphragm and nose become the norm, you won't need reminders, tape, or dilators. You will become a quiet, relaxed, nose breather, and your body will reward you for it. That will be something to celebrate, and you'll have plenty of energy to do so. Your body will receive more oxygen and be less sick. You will start sleeping (and breathing) like a baby.

But what if your nose is clogged? I have fortunate news for you. Unless you have a skeletal problem, a tissue obstruction, or a foreign body like a Lego® stuck up there, the very act of using your nose more will open it. If you can't move any air through a congested nose, then obviously, your mouth will be needed until you are healthy enough. But these occasions should be rare and will increasingly become more so as you practice. There are many articles and videos online showing some natural ways to perform nose unblocking exercises as well as how to use nasal rinses and cleanses. You may need some medicinal help in the beginning, but in time your nose will adapt to the program.

Bonus Fuel & Legal Doping!

But wait, there's more! We have one more gas to discuss, and this one packs a punch. Nitric oxide (NO) is a mighty molecule that is as fascinating as it is beneficial to the human body. This gas, which science is just beginning to understand, is incredible. Nitric oxide's discovery led to a Nobel Prize and resulted in many performance-enhancing drugs and the development of Viagra®. NO boasts significant benefits to our immune system and has impressive effects on sex organs, too. It's a bronchodilator, which means it physically opens airways, allowing for smoother airflow. It is also a vasodilator, which relaxes and widens blood vessels. The opening of veins and arteries increases blood flow, lowers blood pressure, and speeds up muscle recovery and wound healing. Nitric oxide also sterilizes incoming air by killing germs. The gas functions as a natural muscle relaxer and a neurotransmitter too. It can reverse plaque and cholesterol buildup in blood vessels. This stuff is incredible, and you've already learned the natural method to get more of it.

The body naturally produces nitric oxide, and we'd be foolish to allow any of it to go to waste. When our bodies form this super-molecule, guess where it is released? Right into the nose! It accumulates inside the nasal cavity, so if we bypass the nose and breathe through our mouths, we miss out. Nose breathing increases nitric oxide use in the body by five times over mouth breathing! Nasal concentrations of nitric oxide are also higher at lower flow rates. And when we breathe lightly, we carry even more of it into the lungs. If you need more supporting evidence for calm nose breathing, there it is.

Several foods, antioxidants, and dietary supplements can increase NO in the body. For those who want to elevate levels of this wonder-drug, do a little research on ways to boost it through diet. I have tried many food variations and continue to do so. I believe some of them help, but I have no way to measure or validate the results. I can say that I have grown to love beets and dark chocolate. They taste terrible, however, if consumed at the same time.

Humming is another proven, simple hack that also increases nitric oxide production. The high-frequency vibration in our head and chest increases concentrations of the gas five to fifteen times. Many Eastern practices teach exhalation humming and preach that the action makes us more self-aware. People are encouraged to hum, exhale, and focus on bad thoughts leaving the body. I cannot confirm what leaves the body, but I do know what enters. I hum all the time now, not just during meditation time. I hum music when in public and while I work. I only do the classic, deep, monkish "Ohm" when I'm alone so that I don't freak anybody out. I now wonder if perhaps people aren't humming because they are happy. Maybe they are happy because they are humming.

It should be clear now that the goal is to breathe through the nose at all times, using the diaphragm to get air into the lower lungs while maintaining calm breaths. Better efficiency in the lower lungs and more dilated airways will make it possible to move more air with less effort. Since we are no longer over-exhaling and surrendering too much CO_2, we enjoy a better transfer of oxygen into the cells that need it to thrive. We should be doing this all day and ideally, all night too.

Taking It to the Next Level

After incorporating these breathing fundamentals into daily life, we can add one more layer. If committed to mastering our airflow, we also want to maintain this calm, full, breathing during stress and exercise.

Let's look at non-exercise induced stress first. When we get stressed or anxious, our heart rate speeds up, and we begin using our chests to breathe more. Our inhaling and exhaling become louder and faster. This breathing sequence signals to our brain that we are in a stress pattern. The brain releases stress hormones during this type of breathing, which compounds the problem. In this situation, do you think it would be wise to amplify the behavior by doing more of it? Or would it be a better strategy for a self-disciplined, well-trained over-achiever to immediately return to the nose and the diaphragm, and to take slow, calm breaths? We should slow it down, break the pattern, and regain control of both our physiology and our focus. Calm breathing can help diffuse many stressful situations.

When we are exercising, the urge to breathe more kicks in too. This is natural. However, we now understand that we have a plentiful supply of oxygen, and it replenishes faster than we can consume it. So why is the overwhelming urge to breathe more present? It's not starvation for oxygen. Our brain is not in a panic, responding to dropping oxygen levels. The urge to breathe is more of a reaction to a low tolerance for rising CO_2. When muscles are being used, they heat up and produce more carbon dioxide. When CO_2 levels rise, our brain signals us to breathe more because it is sensitive to the CO_2 levels. This increase in breathing drives off more of the rising CO_2. But remember: we need some of that CO_2 to stay there so that, when the oxygen comes by, it can be traded and used in the now taxed tissues. The best time to deliver more oxygen is just after our muscles get worked, stressed, and tired out. During exercise, our heart pumps more blood to move more RBCs faster. If there is enough CO_2 left in the system, the oxygen can be effectively used and consumed.

The way to keep the gases in a more optimal balance and to train our brains to be less sensitive to the rising CO_2 is to learn to maintain the superior breathing techniques at all times. Just like training our biceps to grow and perform at a higher level, we must push through the uncomfortable limits to build strength and tolerance. Through repetition and a little time, we train our systems to be less averse to the buildup of lactic acid (the burn). As this tolerance improves, so do our arms. We must similarly train our breathing. If we resist the urge to gasp and turbo exhale during exercise, our bodies will adapt, get stronger, and build a higher tolerance for CO_2. If we stick with deep, calm, nasal breathing, our brain gets retrained. Our CO_2 tolerance improves, and we can last longer in between breaths without the urge to suck and blow more air.

If you want to measure your CO_2 tolerance levels as they improve, there is an easy way to do so. Patrick McKeown, the renowned Buteyko breathing expert, teaches a simple method to measure this tolerance level. His books and classes teach how to measure the (BOLT) Body Oxygen Level Test without medical equipment. All you need is a timer. To measure your BOLT score, he says to breathe normally for a few minutes. When you are ready to measure your score, exhale the last normal breath out, pinch your nose closed with your fingers, and start the timer. Hold your breath until you feel the first distinct urge to breathe. We are not trying to set a world record or measure a maximum holding time. When the first urge to breathe comes on, note the timer, release your fingers, and resume normal breathing. This may only be eight seconds for some and forty-five for others. McKeown says the optimal time for a well-trained, healthy person who is breathing well is forty seconds. If you keep a log of your BOLT score, you will see this number rise over time as you become a better breather and your CO2 tolerance improves.

For those who want to push to higher levels of CO2 tolerance, high altitude training or breath-holding exercises may be of interest. That sort of training requires adequate instruction and monitoring. McKeown offers an extensive amount of information on these things in his writings, videos, and training programs too.

For everyone else who wants to up their breathing game, the sequence is simple. Start breathing correctly, as laid out in this chapter. Begin doing it at rest, striving to maintain the practice all day and all night. Once the pattern becomes well established, try to use the same techniques during mild physical activity, such as walking. Eventually, work your way up to moderate exercise as your tolerance improves. As your mind and body adapt and get stronger, maybe you can soon challenge Floyd Mayweather to a three-round boxing match with your mouth taped closed. Feel free to send me a 2% commission on your $50 million pay per view deal. When you are preparing for your fight, watch videos of previous matches and notice which athlete starts mouth breathing first and which athlete loses the battle.

Finally, I know some of you over-achievers are wondering if there are reasonable ways to increase your RBC and hemoglobin numbers too. Low RBCs and hemoglobin can cause people to be anemic, which significantly inhibits performance. A simple blood test will test for anemic conditions. If your counts are low, taking iron supplements or increasing iron-rich foods may be warranted. The production of red blood cells is controlled by a hormone called erythropoietin (EPO), which is naturally produced by the kidneys. Adequate production of EPO coincides with healthy levels of protein in our diet. EPO levels can also increase up to 24% by adequately practiced breath-holding exercises. Those exercises require training. I do use some of them, but I think that mastering the fundamentals, as mentioned previously for superior breathing is the best focus. Blood transfusions are the other way to increase EPO and RBCs, as Lance Armstrong can attest. I have never tried those, and I hope you will never need them either. Too much EPO can be very dangerous. The best plan for healthy levels of RBCs and hemoglobin is probably a balanced, whole food diet.

We've covered a lot of material to establish and reinforce a few simple fundamentals. Breathe well as we cruise into the next chapter, humming all the way. You will need the extra oxygen delivery and improved focus for where we are heading.

CHAPTER 4
Better Inputs for Better Output
– Water & Food

W E'VE COVERED HOW we should use our noses. Now it's time to address what to do with our mouths. The topic of food and beverage, which should be simple by nature, has become needlessly complicated in recent years. So many people obsess over obscure, fringe items while ignoring basic standards for eating and drinking that carry massive weight. There's probably a great pun opportunity in there about carrying massive weight, but I'll keep moving as a healthy person should.

H2Ohhh

We've all heard that our bodies are 60% water, but that fact most likely never inspired an aqueous awakening or motivated you to do anything heroic. Regardless of our level of enthusiasm, the H2O molecule is essential for all life. In the human body, the vast majority of metabolic processes and biochemical reactions occur in a watery solution. Without enough water for each reaction, those processes struggle, and our systems suffer. And when our systems aren't working right, there's no way we can perform at a high level. And yet, three-fourths of Americans are dehydrated, despite an abundance of clean, cheap, running water.

I'm a former member of that dried up, poor-performing majority. It wasn't that I was guzzling artificially flavored, aspartame-infused, diet colas all day like most of the addicts around me. Nor was I pounding caffeine and sugar-laced energy drinks in the place of water. If I drank anything other than a morning coffee or an evening primitivo, it was probably water. My problem was not that I was drinking toxic sludge; it was that I wasn't drinking anything at all. My excuse? I wasn't thirsty. When I did consume H2O, it was infrequent and unplanned. It was typical for me to finish an entire meal without ever touching the water glass or finish a full day of work without a single thirsty cue.

Drinking tiny amounts of water and copious amounts of wine and coffee, sweating in the 100-degree Georgia heat, with stress-induced diarrhea a few times per week… What could go wrong? I never considered dehydration as a potential cause of my health issues, but I now realize that my body was continually crying out for water. Unfortunately, I was unfamiliar with the language it was screaming.

When dehydrated, our bodies are in distress, and that leads to a grab bag of unpleasantries:

- Our brain steals the water it needs to survive from our body, leaving all the other organs to wrestle with the deficit.
- Our muscular function and blood circulation are restricted.
- We suffer from memory loss and a lack of concentration.
- Our pH becomes acidic.
- Anxiety levels rise, and we become more irritable
- Inflammation increases, and our bodies get stiff and tired.

- Our immune system is compromised, and we are more susceptible to sickness.
- We take much longer to heal and recover.
- Our system is unable to clear toxic substances and waste products.
- Proper digestion is inhibited.
- Frequent headaches and brain fog set in.
- Our skin and oral cavity become dry.
- Energy levels drop, endurance diminishes, and we age faster.

Think I'm being dramatic? My body manifested every one of these complications, but I was too busy, ignorant, and distracted to notice.

The first thing that doctors should ask after determining how well we are sleeping is how much water we are drinking—and yet I don't think anyone ever asked me about my daily volume intake of water. They didn't even mention it after I handed them a half-filled urine sample jar that more closely resembled pine sap. On second thought, maybe they did ask, and I was too dehydrated to remember. I do recall one occasion when I was donating blood for a charity, and we had to abort the mission halfway through the process because my blood stopped dripping! You would think that not having any more blood to give would be a wake-up call. Instead, the nurses offered me a cola on the way out as consolation. Anybody with a partially hydrated brain knew what needed to happen. It was time to get serious about water.

Drink It Up

The Mayo Clinic recommends 2.7 liters of water per day for women and 3.7 liters for men. Other credible sources say that the correct amount of daily H2O in ounces is equal to 40% to 60% of your body weight in pounds. So, if you weigh 180 pounds, you should probably drink 72 to 108 ounces per day. Individual needs vary with body type, climate, activity levels, age, and other factors such as pregnancy or breastfeeding. But 108 ounces is a lot of water, even if we get much of it through the foods we eat. By any numeric formula for optimal health, I knew I was coming up short on my water intake. I needed around 60 more ounces per day to hit my target. It took almost two weeks of faithfully keeping up my quota before I consistently produced urine that didn't look like anti-freeze. The fluid eventually became clear, as did my negligence. The dramatic results from the supplementation of this life-giving free medicine blew my mind.

Maintaining a water surplus is way easier than recovering from a deficit. Prevention is so simple, which could be why it gets overlooked. Five glasses of water a day reduces the risk of a heart attack by 41%. Drinking water does this! Not receiving kale smoothies through an IV line, soaking naked in a deprivation tank of krill oil, or snorting exotic root extracts; Drinking water! When we have a sinus infection or the flu, we are told to drink plenty of fluids. What if we just stayed hydrated and avoided the sickness altogether? Why wait for the suffering to remember to hydrate? Even in the absence of feeling sick, waiting for your body to tell you it's thirsty is a costly mistake. It's incredible just how fast our bodies can shed water and become dehydrated—just ask a wrestler. When we are short on water, we are short on health. We must be proactive and raise our drinking standards.

Beyond preventing debilitating sickness and disease, hydration has also been proven to impact our mood. Even mild dehydration negatively affects our attitude and energy. When lacking adequate water, our body is under stress and perceives the occurrence as a threat, as it should. Stress hormones and neurotransmitters are released, heightening our anxiety and tension. Fatigue and confusion set in, making it harder for us to execute the tasks in front of us, which only elevates our stress level even more. If we want to maintain a positive mood, we must manage our water. I kept a log for a few months of my daily mood, pH, and water consumption. Not surprisingly, I felt poorly on days when I failed to meet my target volume. This correlated with a drop in pH almost every time. A lower pH meant that my body was more acidic during those times of inadequate water supply. When you consider that a few hours at acidic levels do damage to the body, the thought of maintaining acidity for several days, weeks, or years is scary.

It's possible to have too much water in our bodies, but in modern, high-activity society, it's more likely that we'll have too little than too much. When paramedics load someone into an ambulance, they immediately start fluids and oxygen. Amazingly, these two simple supplements arrest, reverse, and prevent many ailments by themselves. The emergency personnel are not too worried about over-hydration but are gravely concerned with a lack thereof. The key, as always, is to maintain a proper balance of water.

One of the ways our bodies manage the ever-changing water balance is by using electrolytes. Most people have heard of them, but forget they exist. That is, until a sluggish search for them in the drug store after a hangover or a bout of food poisoning. When you see people who don't have kids wandering the pediatric medicine aisle, you know they had a rough night. If you see them also buying diapers, you know it was a really rough night. Give them some space. Adrenalized sports drink commercials tout their electrolyte content, but what are electrolytes anyway? Simply put, they are minerals in the body that produce electrically charged ions when dissolved in water. These electric charges regulate how water moves into and out of our cells via osmosis and influence the health and activities of our nerves, muscles, and other organs, including our brain. They move nutrients into cells, move waste out, and keep our pH in balance. Water must be readily available for those reactions to take place. Without the proper balance of these minerals in solution, our cells would either dry out and whither, or swell up and burst.

Sodium, calcium, potassium, chlorine, phosphate, and magnesium are all commonly found electrolytes supplied by the foods we eat. The levels of electrolytes in the body fluctuate continually depending on activity, diet, and water intake. Goal #1 is to get to ideal levels of water and electrolytes. Goal #2 is to steadily replenish both as they get used and discarded by the body. The amount of water and electrolytes that you take in should equal the amount you are losing through normal biologic processes. Medications, infections, stress, sleep, breathing, diet, vomiting, diarrhea, exercise, sweating, liver issues, or kidney problems can all upset your balance. Normal daily activity can also disrupt the equilibrium if we aren't adequately replenishing our H2O supply. If we lose too many electrolytes or too much water, we end up with lackluster performance.

My lab reports were all over the map, showing that my body was deficient in many of the things I knew I was regularly eating. My potassium level was inadequate, even after eating bananas. My sodium level was low after a bacon breakfast or a Mexican lunch. I was taking a daily multivitamin, and my vitamin C was still deficient. How could this be? Other levels on my reports were high when they should not have been for a healthy person. My blood glucose level elevated some days, even if I didn't eat any sweets. My creatinine and urea levels were high, indicating that my kidneys were not functioning correctly. I was too good for results this bad. As it turned out, my electrolyte and water balance was off. The thing I needed more than any other was plain water and a little salt.

Many of the fluids we drink actually force us to be more

dehydrated, even though they are mostly made up of water. Beverages like coffee, tea, beer, wine, sodas, and energy drinks send us to the bathroom to urinate more often. More water is technically coming into the system when we drink these, sure, but the problem is that they may also require much more of our water stores to remove them from the body properly. We *lose* water and electrolytes when drinking some beverages. That pint of craft IPA may require an additional twenty ounces of pure water to eliminate the alcohol and hops from your system. You've got a lot more drinking to do than you originally anticipated. When I have an alcoholic beverage now, which is an increasingly rarer event, I drink a glass of water beforehand. The 1:1 water to alcohol ratio keeps me more hydrated and also influences me to imbibe less. The more chemicals, flavors, additives, caffeine, sugars, and whatever else are in our drinks, the more water will be required to clear them from our system. Water washes out waste and toxins faster than other drinks, without adding more waste products.

With these concepts in mind, I embarked on a two-step, revolutionary plan for a month.

Step 1: Eliminate all beverages that are not water

Step 2: Drink more water

Groundbreaking, right?

I gave up my daily alcohol and coffee for an entire month. That was tough, especially the first week. I was addicted to both and had been consuming them regularly for years. I had intense withdrawal symptoms from the coffee cessation; I craved caffeine and the sweet creamer I added to it every day. I was an angry zombie with a pounding headache for a few days. Not drinking in the evening wasn't too hard, but it seemed to make me a little paranoid and jittery for a few days. Thankfully, humans are very adaptable. Once you establish a proper sleep rhythm, you no longer need stimulants for waking or depressants for winding down. It just takes about ten days to convince your body of it. I started drinking more water every day, all day. Upon waking each morning, I drank a glass of water, which increases metabolism. On the first glass of the day, I also stirred in a little Himalayan sea salt to replenish electrolytes and trace minerals. For most everyone, the most prolonged period of the day without water is when we sleep. Our bodies still use water while resting and recovering, so we wake in a deficit and should replenish.

I committed to consuming additional water every two hours of my day to hit my goal. This required digital reminders and visual cues because I didn't feel thirsty. Incremental, consistent intake is superior to big gulps. I also made it a standard practice to drink a full glass before each meal. The modifications felt great. As it turns out, many times, when our bodies are hungry and motivate us to eat, what they crave is water. If your body learns that you can't be trusted to drink enough water, it increases your appetite to ensure the necessary water arrives through food. Before I became adequately hydrated, I was always hungry. When my voracious appetite normalized as I drank more water, I realized I had been confusing hunger with thirst.

The prescription here isn't complicated. Drink plenty of water, and drink less of everything else. I say go all in, cold turkey! Drop everything that isn't water for a few weeks. Take your reusable bottle with you wherever you go. This will serve as a reminder to drink more and eliminate tons of waste and expense from buying disposable containers. If you dislike drinking water, use some natural flavoring to get the habit going. You could infuse fruit or add some all-natural, concentrated drops. There are dozens of flavors available to give you some variety and prevent boredom. In time, your body will reward you for your intelligent efforts, and you won't need the flavoring to enjoy a glass. Cucumber is one of my favorite infusion options. Mint leaves or lemon are also classics.

Remember: steady, consistent replenishment all day is best. Guzzling twenty-four ounces in one shot is inferior to taking in the same volume in smaller increments over several hours. If you have some testing done and find out that your electrolytes are low, get hydrated first, then supplement with real, natural, whole foods like spinach, beans, avocados, oranges, soybeans, or bananas. Be aware that many popular diets contribute to electrolyte deficiency. If you are exercising for an hour or less, drinking plain water is probably sufficient. If you are playing in a tennis tournament all day long or running a marathon for five hours, electrolyte supplements are likely a good idea for the temporary deficit.

Of all the behavioral modification in this book, drinking adequate water is probably the easiest. It's cheap and readily available. Drink enough water, plain and simple. Your entire system will appreciate it, and your mood will reflect the improvements.

Nom Nom Nom

This book is about wellness, so we must discuss food, but we'll make it quick. There are tens of thousands of books about food and nutrition. Some are useful. Many contradict each other, and others are flat out dangerous. Every year there are new fads, diets, and programs aimed at helping people lose weight, detox, and feel better. There is always a market for these materials because we repeatedly get into body and diet trouble, thanks to convenience, negligence, emotional instability, laziness, and a host of other factors.

Many aspects of our food system are unhealthy and corrupt. Many food items are intentionally designed to create dependency and addictions, not to create optimal health. Sadly, our healthcare system seems to be complicit in many

65

ways. As a society, we have strayed from healthy living in almost every aspect of life because of trends, marketing, profits, and consumer behavior. As individuals, we must be willing to be the one percent and lead a contrarian life in whatever way necessary. When it comes to what we eat, we should buck the norms associated with food. Look around. The results from following the masses are painfully apparent. Perhaps, for the first time in human civilization, entire nations of people are dying of malnutrition in the presence of excess food. A lack of adequate nutrition is contributing to the further breakdown of bodily systems and results in more pain, anxiety, depression, and poor performance.

The human body has an incredible ability to heal and to meet our daily needs if we put the right food into it. We need a long-term, permanent plan to raise the standards for what we eat. Another crash diet won't suffice. Proper eating is a lifestyle, not a temporary rescue. The main food rule for this book is simple and to the point:

Eat real food!

It's that easy. If we stop eating manufactured, overly processed, "foodish" substances, and begin to eat real food, we can rise out of nutritional poverty. By real food, I mean food solely derived from ingredients that the earth naturally provides. Not only is much of what we eat devoid of any nutritional value, but it's loaded with potentially harmful things. So many of the ingredients in our food products have no business in the human body. Our systems are not equipped to process many of the lab-made chemicals present in our food system. Our bodies get confused by the foreign molecules that we swallow, often reacting violently to their presence. We are just beginning to understand how these microscopic foreign bodies are wreaking havoc on our natural biological processes.

- Should we be ingesting artificial flavors, colors, preservatives, and sweeteners?

- How are these chemical compounds even made?
- How is this stuff processed in the body?
- Do the meats and vegetables we consume contain pesticides, antibiotics, fungi, bacteria, or toxic compounds?
- Should we be consuming food that has been strategically manipulated to make us more addicted to it?
- Do we even care what type of fuel we are burning in the only body that we have?

Wake up! We are too good to eat this bad.

My household switched to an all-natural diet many years ago out of necessity. We were grasping for anything that would help to manage autism spectrum disorder in one of our children. We tried many behavioral modifications and several types of ongoing therapy. We used a host of supplements and medications. But ultimately, we found that the most impactful changes came when we did subtraction instead of addition. Removing many of the items found in the modern family diet showed undeniable positive results for all of us. We thought we were eating well before because we avoided typical junk foods and drinks. We thought "fat-free" and "reduced fat" meant "healthy." We were mistaken.

Our family eliminated all the over-processed, chemical-laden ingredients. It was inconvenient and took some time to master, but everyone benefited from the extra discipline. We bought nothing but all-natural groceries. We started growing many of our own fruits and vegetables. When we ate meat, it was typically some form of wild game that I harvested myself. Every food ingredient in our home now either grew out of dirt or had a mother. Over the past eight years, it has become substantially easier to find healthier foods because the industry is waking up to the issues, and consumers are demanding better options. You don't have to bring in a load of organic garden soil or rig a fishing pole to get real food—but if that is required to get the right food into your body, do it.

Many people rant about not being able to afford organic foods or smarter options. Others talk about how inconvenient it is to cook and spend extra time preparing real food. I like to remind them that taking four prescription drugs, giving yourself daily injections, and having triple bypass surgery is expensive and rather inconvenient too. How much does it cost to miss a week of work due to getting sick? Besides, most fruits, nuts, and vegetables are better without any cooking. It doesn't get much more convenient than that.

The Lifestyle Food Plan

I know you aren't a member of the "that must be nice" crowd, willing to remain a helpless, unconscious victim of the food industry. Nonetheless, it may be time for some adjustments. I want to suggest an uncomplicated, five-part plan.

1 - Buy the best available option.

There are so many options now for what we eat. I'd wager that you can find an organic or at least a natural version of almost everything you like. You can buy pickles with three ingredients: cucumber, vinegar, and salt, or you can opt for the ones swimming in yellow dye. (You could also easily make them at home.) We can buy dark brown bread that is made to look healthier by adding chemical preservatives and artificial caramel coloring. Or we could pick up the more straightforward option without all the additives. The same goes for the meats we buy. If you can't pronounce nine of the five-syllable ingredients listed on the label, it's probably not the best option. 5-methyl, 2-headed, buta-beefalin does not occur in nature. Whether there are two options or eight, choose the best one available. Shop around or venture down other aisles. Many foods on the shelf have a cleaner version in the frozen section. Compare labels and choose wisely. It may cost a bit more to get a healthier version, but it must become a way of life. Tastes and budgets can adjust in time. Standards must come first.

2 – Eat whole, natural foods.

Fruits and vegetables are usually better when consumed raw; the way nature produces them. Know that many things that come in a non-refrigerated box or bag are full of chemicals added to prevent caking, preserve freshness, or prevent decomposition. Avoid artificial colors, flavors, preservatives, and sweeteners. Excess sugar, including high fructose corn syrup, is out too. As a society, we are addicted to sugar, and the food companies know it. They are happy to make you dependent on their products by adding copious amounts of sugar. Shopping the perimeter of the store is generally much healthier than the center aisles where the highly processed food sits. And don't let "convenience" derail your goals. Plan the week ahead of time and prepare for proper nutrition to avoid problems associated with the need for rushed convenience. Fruit, nuts, and veggies are easy to grab and go.

3- Cheating Fairly

For six days per week, follow the plan flawlessly, and don't cheat. On day seven, eat whatever you desire.

Many of us have significant emotional attachments associated with food, so in the beginning, it may be necessary to have a system that doesn't feel like punishment. If you need one, establish a cheat day—*one cheat day!* Having a single day to cheat allows you an emotional benefit, but also keeps your body on track for most of the week. In time, you will feel so noticeably lousy after the cheat day that you may no longer want it. You can also opt for an occasional cheat meal instead of a whole day. One of my guilty pleasures is a piece of southern fried chicken, and I reserve it for Sunday. I know that I will be tired a few hours after I eat it, but sometimes (and only sometimes) I elect to make that trade.

Once you establish your cheat day, do not negotiate, trade days, or make exceptions. The day you pick should be rigid and immovable. If you miss it, it's gone. No IOU's or "saving up" allowed.

4 – Be diverse in what you eat.

Our bodies need nutritional diversity. We should not eat the same foods all year long. Most people unconsciously pick up the same items at the grocery store each week, sticking to the favorite foods out of habit. We order the same few items on the menu from the same few restaurants too. That's a mistake (and another instance of convenience overriding intelligence). Our systems thrive from biodiversity in our diet. Overeating the same things over time can cause damage and imbalance. If we think about evolutionary history, we should assume that our bodies are not meant to eat avocados for fifty-two weeks straight or pound blueberries with every breakfast. Nature provides food in seasons, which is how we should consume them. Overexposure to certain foods can produce a harmful sensitivity to them. In a world of convenient, cheap, trans-global groceries, we need a conscious plan to mix it up. Trying new foods is a great way to create novelty and add some excitement too. Change it up and keep it moving.

5 - Maintain consistent eating schedules.

Many of us have sporadic eating habits because of poor planning, hectic schedules, busyness, and a lack of discipline. We find ourselves stuck for long periods of the day without food and water. Then we binge on a massive meal when we finally get the opportunity. This irregularity confuses our system and hinders proper biorhythms. In doing this, we are training our bodies not to trust us. Our metabolism slows down, and our body begins to store more fat to prepare for these times of starvation. The fat deposits collect in various places throughout the body as backup fuel to burn when food isn't available. Rarely does it accumulate in a flattering manner. If we regularly eat the right foods on a consistent schedule, our metabolism stays high, and we store less fat.

Portion control is essential, but so is frequency. Regular, small, real-food meals throughout the day are a proven way to maintain energy and a better mood. Eating smart is much easier when we aren't desperate for fuel. We get irrational and irritated when our bodies are in distress. In contrast, when eating the right foods on a consistent schedule, we avoid much of the stress and anxiety that comes from these panic responses.

That's enough for the five-point food plan. You understand this stuff. Just do it. I recommend you start by going all-natural, all plant-based for two weeks straight. This practice, alone, has an amazing detoxifying and energizing effect.

Extreme Ownership

When you can muster a bold moment of extreme courage, throw out everything in your fridge and in the pantry that isn't real wholesome food, and never replace it. Do not repurchase it in a depressed binge after a hard day. Make it a lifestyle to keep nothing in your home that hurts your body. If it's not in the house, it's no longer a temptation and can't be your crutch. Go elsewhere for your cheat day and make it a celebration. Treats are for birthdays and cheat days, not daily life. Too many will make you spoiled and soft anyway, in more ways than one.

These methods are more accessible and sustainable than some fad diet. They also allow you to eliminate the guilt, stress, and anxiety associated with food decisions. Try it out and jumpstart your body transition. After two weeks, grab a bowl of natural ice cream with nitrate-free bacon on top to celebrate. Keep the plan simple, and also the foods.

If you need some motivation before attacking your fridge and purging your pantry, spend some time thinking about how you want to live in another ten, twenty, or thirty years. Take charge of your health and wellbeing. No one can do it for you. Lay out all of your medicines and think about life with more of them and life without them. Look through some old photos or spend a few minutes in front of the mirror naked. Discuss the plan with yourself aloud. Determine who all of this stuff is for. Establish who wins and who loses from your action or inaction. Then make the choice you know is right. You are too good to eat this bad.

CHAPTER 5
Strain, Pain, & Gains - Exercise

I T WOULD BE an injustice to have a book about wellness, stress, and anxiety and fail to discuss exercise. But there is no need to get carried away on this one. Let's keep the physical part simple with a two-part criterion:

1. Work up a good sweat at least three times per week.

   Sex and yardwork count. (Don't do those at the same time).

   Night sweats and eating hot wings do not count. (Don't do those at the same time either.)

2. Push or pull something heavy at least two days per week.

   Some form of weight training or other activity that requires muscular strain is required. Push yourself to your limit. It's supposed to burn. Work a muscle safely to the extreme, then allow at least three days of recovery before working that same muscle again.

That's it! If you want to lose a bunch of weight or bulk up, you will need to do more than this. If it's energy, good sleep, and clear thinking you're after, this Rx will do it. It will only stink for two weeks; then it will get much easier. Stop making it needlessly complicated. Just keep showing up.

Work it!

CHAPTER 6
Motion & Emotion
– The Mind/Body Connection

THERE IS NO clear delineation marking where physiology stops and psychology starts in real life. The mind and body are permanently tethered and constantly coordinating. Our existence and performance are a product of that inseparable blend, and it would be prudent to keep that in mind moving forward.

You've made it through several of the physical components necessary for making lasting, positive changes. But those fundamentals are only elementary steps in the overall process. Those first few chapters are likely the easiest to understand and to implement. We can now transition from the physiological to the psychological, a space that may feel like foreign territory to you and where an entirely different kind of work is required. Hold on to your hats. We are about to pick up the intensity and shake things up.

Personal Paradigms

The key to genuine human progress is not just personal knowledge or consuming insightful information. It's becoming a person capable of breaking old patterns and building new habits. That is a challenge because the human brain is wired to repeat behaviors. The more we do something, the more established the neural connections become in our systems, and the more likely we are to do them again. So many of the actions and reactions we experience later in life are autonomic. They are mindless repetitions and reflexes based on previously established patterns. The paradoxical problem is that some of these behaviors once served a critical purpose (and probably served us well) but are no longer needed. The leftover patterns are now sticking around for one simple reason: we have not replaced them. Some of these old patterns are holding us back, limiting our potential to experience life on another level.

Here's a basic example from my life: When I was in grade school, I was always the smallest person in my classes. That made me feel weak, vulnerable, and less valuable, and I developed resentment and anger toward bigger kids who picked on me. I became aggressive. I learned to strike first, both verbally and physically. This behavior lasted years, and parts of it ended up spilling over into high school, college, and even into adult life. Aggression was a necessary survival skill; it protected me. The problem was that as the years went on, acting this way was no longer necessary or useful. No one was picking on me anymore.

My protective hostility became a severe setback. My leftover resentful attitude, coupled with a compulsive need to take up more space in the room, was damaging my relationships. I had no humility. I was always in a hurry to prove myself, whether casually meeting new friends over a beer or speaking on stage to several hundred professionals. The longstanding pattern hurt my progress in life because I was still operating in the old model. There was nothing I needed to prove, but I still had a chip on my shoulder. I'm not sure when a behavior or attitude becomes part of your identity and character, but I had far surpassed that point. It wasn't until I had the education to recognize that I no longer needed such self-protection that I could then gather the tools to dismantle it and replace it with something better.

Even if the reasoning behind our patterns made sense at one time, many of our emotions and behaviors may no longer be necessary or are rarely needed. Things like resentment, jealousy, greed, dominance, paranoia, fear, anger, depression, and anxiety can stick around way too long. These sentiments are usually longstanding micro-patterns spilled over from macro issues from long ago. In most cases, it's an unfortunate reality that our bodies prefer to repeat old patterns and keep reacting the same way we always have. Lucky for us, it doesn't have to be this way, though. They are not permanent diseases. Rewriting history isn't required to break a longstanding habit, and you don't need to lie on a leather sofa and talk with a stranger about your childhood to get the process of change started.

One of the most valuable skills we can cultivate in daily life is the ability to recognize when we are in a foolish pattern. Honest awareness should come before any action. Once in sight, we can craft the discipline needed to break destructive patterns. Some of our patterns require days, if not years, to fully excavate, discern, and dissolve. But fortunately, there are many behaviors that can be broken in an instant. We have the ability to change unfavorable situations and initiate new cycles quickly. We can guard against damaging states and weak emotional tendencies and attack them when identified. Through discovery, creativity, and new actions, we can develop new wired connections to new areas of the brain and create new patterns. Over time, repetition strengthens these connections, making the behaviors easier to keep around without such a grueling effort.

The Undeniable Power of State

Most of our behaviors are driven by emotions. But the thing that greatly influences our emotions is our state. Interpretations, decisions, and actions are direct results of our present state. It determines how we see, what we hear, and how we feel. Attempting to change behaviors is not just a matter of reason or willpower. If that were the case, we wouldn't be in the position we are in. Many of our behavioral and emotional patterns are connected to our state. They are a package deal. We need to develop a way to take control of our state so that we can move more efficiently and accomplish difficult tasks.

When I refer to the state, I mean the current, real-time conditions involving both our physical bodies and our mental processes. Our mood is a key indicator of our current state and something we should never allow to go unnoticed. But our state involves more than just our mood or current attitude. We may falsely think that our state results from our environment or blind happenstance. But we are not just victims or bystanders with no choice.

When we are in a positive state, we process and respond to an event in one way, but if we are in a negative state, we react differently to the same stimulus. Our perception differs based on our emotional state. Why do we continually wander away from this inherent truth? How we see, hear, and feel is mostly determined by our state. If we are exhausted, we perform on a different level than when we are well-rested. When we are angry, we respond more negatively than when we are joyful. When we feel powerful, our performance varies from when we feel broken or weak. This phenomenon is no secret, but we forget about it too often. The way we receive information, give it meaning, and make decisions depend heavily on our current state.

For instance, Woman A is feeling insecure and jealous.

Woman B, who also happens to be very attractive, enters the scene and smiles at Woman A's man. This simple action triggers an infuriating response. Is this a legitimate threatening situation, or an explosive result of a poor state affecting her thinking? Furthermore, if Woman A is in a negative state, her man may get punished for being charming and handsome, which is what she liked about him in the first place. In contrast, if Woman A were in a confident, satisfied, secure, playful state, she could see the exact same gesture as a compliment or validation. The same event could produce more affection and intimacy if the players are in an optimal state.

Let's consider another scenario. A man is leaving the stadium after his team lost the championship. He's dejected, embarrassed, angry at the refs, and frustrated with his team. He does this after every loss. A rival fan passes him in the parking lot, raises his hand to offer a high five, and says, "Good game, dude." What happens? To someone in a poor state, this could be an invitation to fight. To another fan who was in a positive state, enjoyed the game, and thought it was fair, the same gesture could make his day even better. In any of these cases, these people have been in these states before. They will proceed to run the most familiar pattern. These scenarios remind me of a quote by the Greek philosopher Epictetus: "Any person capable of angering you becomes your master."

A more serious example that illustrates these points is what happened on September 11, 2001. The entire world watched in disbelief as the terror attacks unfolded. Those in NYC viewed the real-time events across the city skyline, and the rest of us viewed the horrid, live news feeds. We all saw the same scene. How people responded to that same spectacle was very different, though. People who were in a state of anger became enraged, eager to wage war. People who were afraid grew more terrified, wondering what would come next. Those in a sad place became more heartbroken, mourning the tragedies. Charitable people donated money, blood, living spaces, and time; courageous heroes sprang into action, and grateful people squeezed their loved ones tighter. The reactions were wide-ranging, but I would like to suggest that most of us may have been merely running our standard patterns. Once again, our state determined our response.

We can easily appreciate how our current state influences us, but another important variable to consider is how our current state directly affects the people around us. It's reckless, costly, and selfish not to be conscious of this. I yell at my kids, and others kick their dog because of something that happened hours earlier that altered our state. Ignoring the reality that how we feel dramatically influences the people and situations around us is irresponsible. Whether fantastic or terrible, there is no denying that states are contagious. We tend to behave similarly to others around us. This can either be dangerous or redeeming. A mob can destroy lives, and a tribe can save them. We are all capable of both extremes.

We naturally gravitate to people in higher states. It's only after longstanding patterns of anger and sadness that we intentionally seek out a poorly performing group in which to commiserate. One attitude lifts our spirits and has the potential to elevate us. The opposite one reinforces the damaging pattern.

Think for a minute. How do you view someone who is a downer, drama queen, or a pessimist?

In contrast, how do you feel about the person you know who lives in a positive state? Who would you rather hang out with? Again, it's natural to want to be near this type of energy. It's attractive. But when we begin to resent positivity in others, we must recognize that we are in serious trouble ourselves.

Body and Mind

Have you ever noticed that there is a universal body language to communicate certain moods? You may have never thought about it in these terms, but let's highlight a favorite, familiar, well-practiced state. Regardless of geography, culture, language, age, or economic status, people project consistent signals for being depressed. What do you see when others are depressed? What do you do yourself when you are there?

First, the body: Your shoulders drop, shrinking forward. You lower your head more than usual. You breathe shallower as energy levels sink. You speak with a softer, more lethargic tone and even blink slower. If you are sitting, you slouch. If you are standing, you hunch over. Biochemically, hormones and receptors are changing rapidly and signaling your brain to be depressed and to follow the usual pattern. Humans do this, whether they are three or eighty-three. My kids do it, and no one ever even taught them, or maybe I did inadvertently.

Next, the mind: When depression is present, our thinking consistently follows patterns too. We probably think about everything that is wrong instead of what is right. We think about what we don't have instead of what we have. We dwell on the past more than the future and on things we cannot control instead of those that we can. Why? Well, a more in-depth answer will come in a later chapter, but for now, the reason is simple: it's a familiar pattern, one we have practiced before and find easy to repeat. We do this with many moods, situations, and states.

My question for you to ponder is impactful: Do you think our emotional mood prompts the physical changes in the body, or do the physical body changes affect the mind and mood? The answer: Both! Either one can initiate or intensify the other. This concept is empowering to understand because it places you back into the driver's seat. We don't have to be helpless passengers on a crazy ride. Not only can we prevent a bad mood from escalating, but we can also stop it, or better still, reverse it. If the body and the mind have such a powerful influence over our decision making, we should craft a plan to use both. For practicality, we'll need to separate the two. We'll start with the body, then proceed to the mind. It's much easier than you think.

Body Control - Phase 1

We will dive into some psychological elements later. For this moment, let's focus solely on physiology. What do you suspect would happen if when you felt depressed, you consciously moved your body in a different pattern? What if you were rebellious, abandoned the common tendencies, and disrupted the pattern instead? What if you stood up straight, aligned your spine, poked out your chest, raised your chin, fixed your gaze upward, breathed deeply, spoke boldly, and moved with higher energy and purpose? I can tell you what would happen. You would break a pattern. You would have a better experience than before by influencing your system to go in a different direction. Even if you know it's a trick, you will still break the pattern. Think this sounds too easy? So did I, but I was willing to test it out anyway.

In a recent study at Harvard, researchers studied the compelling influence of posture. Subjects in the experiment had no idea what was to be measured. After obtaining baseline lab work, the participants were given poses to emulate. One half of the group held high-power poses (standing like Superman), and the other half maintained low-power poses (slumping in a desk chair). After just two minutes of postural changes, the results were quite impressive.

The group using high-power poses reported feeling stronger and performed better in mock interviews than the other group. They were also more likely to take risks than the other group. But those are just subjective measures of mood. What about their actual body chemistry? The power posing group decreased their cortisol levels (stress hormones) around 25% and increased testosterone by about 19%. Testosterone is a hormone that regulates fat, muscle, and red blood cell production. It also determines your sex drive, fertility, and your mood.

In contrast, low-power poses increased cortisol levels by about 17% and decreased testosterone around 10%. That's a 32% difference between groups in cortisol and a 29% difference in testosterone after posing for two minutes! That's two minutes, no drugs, zero cost, and a 30% improvement!

How could anyone possibly understand this knowledge and not immediately start using it? Try it yourself. No, not later; right now. Stand up. Poke out your chest and flash a big grin, showing as many teeth as possible. Clench each fist tightly and pump both arms quickly and powerfully into the air three times. Do it as if you just sank a long putt to win the Masters, or just finished playing the last song at your concert in front of 40,000 adoring fans. Leave your hands up in the air for a moment and smile. Soak it in. Go ahead. I'll wait.

How do you feel after a few seconds of action?

Body position is a dynamic starting place for breaking patterns. I will not bore you with all the studies about the benefits of spine alignment, good posture, stretching, and other physical activities. Just know that body position and movement affect just about everything. That is the case for how much oxygen gets to your brain, how well toxic waste products make it to the exit door, and everything in between. Posture is powerful, and it's a key influencer for changing your overall state.

If we intend to give some respect and attention to the power of our physiology, we need a tactical system for using it well. The one I am recommending is simple. It involves three practical steps:

Step 1: Recognize the poor state.

Step 2: Break the pattern as soon as possible, by whatever means necessary.

Step 3: Practice these changes until they become habits so that we stay out of trouble.

Step 1 requires us to monitor our state continuously. It's imperative to notice when we are in a troublesome spot. This sounds easy, but the adage is true: Old habits are hard to break. Recognizing the inferior state can be uncomfortable in the beginning because it forces us to swallow our pride and admit to mistakes. It becomes easier over time. Awareness is critical, and it requires frequent checks. Let's not forget that longstanding patterns are routine and mostly unconscious. They can easily go unnoticed. We need a backup strategy for when the pattern is not severe enough to trigger any self-awareness. Adding notifications and reminders to your phone or calendar for a self-check may be warranted. A few minutes taken to assess the current state is never wasted. Once per day may be adequate for some, and once per hour may still be insufficient for others.

The only way to effectively evaluate whether or not our state is favorable is to establish the parameters. *What do you want?* That is not a hypothetical question. It requires an answer. What do you want? In what state do you desire to live? What would be best for you? How do you want to feel? What is your goal? What is minimally acceptable? What is optimal? We must know our outcome so we can monitor, adjust, and maintain the right state. I know you are ready to plow through this material, but take a few minutes right now to pause and think specifically about what you sincerely want.

Once you have some framework for what you want, take the next step. Take a few more minutes to imagine what life would be like living in a beautiful, purposeful, powerful state.

How would work feel? How would playing in this realm feel? How would the people you love the most benefit from and respond to this state?

Conversely, how much of the typical day do you spend in a poor state? How has this affected your progress and your relationships? Do not continue to allow old patterns to strip you of who you are meant to be. Some people suffer permanently, living in toxic environments. For me, it was easy to see and feel the positive states, but the poor ones were less obvious. That's because my weak physiology had become routine for me. I felt like I maintained more positivity than the folks around me, but that was a foolish baseline to measure. Now, after a few years of practicing state management, I recognize my deficiencies on a much broader and more accurate scale.

For now, the goal is to recognize when we are in a suboptimal state. We will get into the why of it all later, which is crucial too. We are merely developing awareness in this early stage. We must notice when we are trapped. People can easily spend hours, days, or even years in a lousy state and never realize it. Honest consciousness of what we are feeling is an invaluable skill that few people ever develop.

Step 2 is about taking action. How do we accomplish the goal of breaking the pattern? I'm not referring to some power-of-positive-thinking fodder. Repeating the mantra, "I am not going broke. I am rich." will not stop your past-due creditors from garnishing your wages. We can't just pretend that bad things are not happening. They are happening and will continue to happen. Please allow me to be clear on this. The goal at this stage is not to solve the actual problem. Those solutions come later. The initial intent is simply to break the pattern. We must stop the old program from running on your hard drive. We must take immediate, deliberate, and robust action as soon as we recognize the negative state.

State-changing and pattern-breaking may look different for

each individual, based on where they are and what is available. Stay with me and seriously consider these methods, even though some may sound ridiculous. As soon as we recognize that we are entering or dwelling within a bad state, we need to move. Sometimes a simple change in scenery, sensory input, or both will do the trick. I like to take off my shoes and walk outside. Never underestimate the power of sunlight, fresh air, or a rainstorm.

At other times when I recognize the detrimental state, I instantaneously bolt out the door and sprint down the street as fast as I can. (Pets have no idea how to respond to this one.) If I am alone in my car, I may roll down the windows, blast some hip hop, and rap like it's my job. You know you've done it too. Music is a curiously powerful state changer, which is why it finds a place in cultural and religious ceremonies throughout history. It's easy to dance your way out of a poor state, even if you have two left feet. Other times I perform squats or repeatedly jump as high as I can. I drop and crank out push-ups until failure.

I sometimes open the back door to the house and scream. (I have no clue what the neighbors think of this one.) I shadow box, jump on the trampoline, clap my hands, beat my chest, or speak incantations in loud, funny accents. I jump into a cold shower or the lake. A sudden, obnoxious, Rick Flair "Woo!" works wonders. Whatever it takes, before I can talk myself out of it, I do it. The important thing to do is something. Just do it. Don't overthink it. You know that mad swatting and spitting thing you do when you walk into a spider web or a bug buzzes by your ear? That's the type of aversion reaction we should have when realizing we just wandered into a negative state.

If you are in an environment when acting like a baboon on steroids and methamphetamines is not an option, change something. Use whatever is at your disposal, including sights, smells, breathing, movement, and body position. If nothing else, at least sit up straight or stand tall. Put your shoulders back, open your eyes wide, and take a few conscious and controlled breaths. I know what you are thinking—that this stuff is a little out there for you. I felt that way too. All it takes is a single moment of fortitude and action to become a believer. Soon enough, you will develop a particular affinity for your state-altering activities.

A quick disclaimer: I am officially only recommending legal, safe, healthy means to accomplish state changes. After all, snorting cocaine, setting your neighbor's car on fire, or running naked through Chipotle with ghost peppers taped to your nipples would accomplish a state change too.

Small moments, whether accidental or deliberate, can be transformational. It's proven that even a fake smile or pretend laugh can immediately change your brain chemistry. It's almost impossible to stay angry or depressed when you confuse your system in these ways. When the muscles in your face produce a smile, they signal to your brain that you are happier. Even holding a pencil in your teeth, which creates an expression similar to a smile, has been shown to produce positive effects on your brain. This is bizarre but useful. There is no good reason not to grin like the Cheshire Cat, even if it's fake. Well, except for the fact that you momentarily look like a psychopath. If in public, excuse yourself to the restroom, or hide your face behind a napkin or a book.

Similarly, if you maintain an obnoxious, pretend laugh long enough, it will probably turn into a genuine one. Trust me, this stuff works. It sounds corny, but it's faster and more potent than any drug you could take. It's also free! So, the next moment when you have the awareness and insight that you are in an unfavorable state, change as many variables as you can and do so immediately. Once the pattern breaks and your state changes, then you can work on real solutions and strategies.

Regardless of what the poor state may be or how severe, we must learn to fend it off. We need the ability to process and recalibrate before responding to life's many provocations. A premature, unplanned, emotional response can cost us so much more than the cheap and fleeting satisfaction of expressing our feelings at the moment. We inevitably will fall into some temporary, lousy states. We don't need to stay there. Get out and get out fast! Sometimes this movement will feel effortless as you dance your way out with a smile. Other times it can be more like clawing your way out of a suffocating and crushing avalanche.

Step 3 is simple. Keep practicing until new patterns form and habits are firmly ingrained in your system. Mastery of any type requires focus and repetition. Over time, you will notice when a state change is needed. You will also develop more efficient ways to accomplish it. We must learn to construct new patterns and deconstruct old ones. In the beginning, doing anything contrary to what you would typically do in a poor state is progress. Keep adding to your skill set and hone these practices. Put many items in your bag of tricks and test them out. Be creative. Once we initiate action, the benefits arrive quickly. You will appreciate the differences as time moves on, and the changes will no longer feel like work. They will become a delightful privilege.

A valuable tip for accomplishing these steps is to recruit someone to help you stay on top of things. Only someone who wants the best for you should occupy this role, someone you would give exclusive permission to hit you while you are down. There is a fine line between welcomed accountability and biting criticism. Remember, we only need help when stuck in the wrong pattern. Coincidentally, that is also the time when we are the most volatile and least reasonable. Be careful. It can be treacherous territory.

The person you select needs to be someone you respect. The wrong tone and attitude can make things worse, even if the intent is pure. Some people may need a militant, hard-nosed trainer to get in their face. Others are better served by a gentle, sympathetic nudge in the right direction. I have a select few buddies that can call me out and bluntly tell me when I'm failing to be my best. That permission is mutual. My spouse often provides support by offering me a few minutes alone to recover the proper mood. When I'm disgusted, angry, depressed, or fearful, there are very few people that I want pointing out my negligence and selfishness. However, when I am feeling a little blue, someone I value and admire can assist in the critical phase of recognition. I desire to be my best and want to make them proud too.

Just know that in the beginning stages of learning the craft, it can be especially productive to have someone on your team. Once you become practiced and proficient, you will self-police much better and likely notice the downturn before anyone else could. More often than not, my wife now recognizes that I have made a change instead of asserting that I need one. If you do select an accountability partner in your home, work, or social life, choose wisely.

Mind Control – Phase 2

A successful state change requires two distinct phases. Phase one involves changing the physical body components. You now have some ideas for that. Once we accomplish a physiological pivot, it's necessary to use the newfound momentum to take subsequent actions to propel into phase two. Fortunately, there will now be more energy and vigor to do so. We will need all of it to move to the next strategy. Energy is power. We must harness energy to do hard things. Without it, we are trapped and wounded. I'm not referring to mystical, Deepak Chopra and Eckhart Tolle energy. I'm talking about old school energy, the kind Gatorade sells. With a newly increased boost of energy from a physiological change, it's time to move to the next phase. We must now address our focus. We must learn how to quickly and voluntarily change our thinking to regain control of our minds.

Simply put, we feel what we focus on. This premise is easy to understand and impossible to refute. When we focus on hurtful things, we tend to feel more bothered. If we focus on happier things, we start feeling lighter. Thankfully, we don't have to wonder or guess what we are focused on. All we have to do is pay attention for two seconds. Our thoughts are right in front of us, and they are also a choice. We may have a learned pattern for where our mind automatically goes, but make no mistake: it is a choice. Focus is arguably more challenging to learn to change than posture and movement, but it becomes easier over time.

First, we take inventory and get a baseline measurement by asking probing questions:

- Where are we on the thought spectrum?
- What are we focused on?
- Is it what we have or what we don't have?
- Is it the past or the future?
- Is it what we hate or what we love?
- Is it self-pity and pain or gratitude and joy?
- Is it what we can't control, or what we can?
- Is it fear, anger, and resentment, or courage, strength, and forgiveness?

I never said these things were easy. I said they were a choice.

Before the gift of my recent pivot and awakening, I was a train wreck when it came to my focus. If fifty things were beautiful, I had a knack for focusing on the three things that were not. Tiny items could blow me off track and destroy my mood. It's not that I didn't see the great stuff. I just quickly moved past them and gave most of my attention to the junk. I did it while at work and in the home. With no awareness of my tendencies, my mind would race, scouring the landscape to see what was wrong. I would silently blame the people I thought were lackadaisically responsible for the problems. My sour attitude then led to a sour stomach.

I was discontent with so many things and was too blind to see that my focus was directly congruent with my disgusted attitude. It's shameful looking back at it. I could host forty awesome people at a party but let the two people who canceled at the last-minute ruin my attitude. My irresponsible state tainted many lovely things and stole joy from other people. I missed out on some beautiful experiences by focusing on the wrong details.

I always felt trapped at work, even though I had a more favorable work schedule than any person I knew. I perpetually had a list in my mind of things that needed attention, and there was always urgency associated with getting them done. If an unplanned conversation ran long or a natural setback threatened my plans, my frustration level would elevate and stay high all day. I was always disappointed in other people around me. I resented them when I determined they were lazy, not carrying their weight, or not paying attention. I was discontent and bitter inside, expecting things never to change. I had unhealthy, unrealistic expectations of my peers, staff members, and my family. I could say the same for politicians and professionals too. I simultaneously had too low expectations for myself. I stayed anxious and irritated, although most people never knew it. Negativity was my default state of mind. My lousy posture followed the cues from my weak thinking, causing more back and neck inflammation, which made my mood worse. Remember: If you run into a jerk in the morning, you ran into one jerk. If you run into them all day, every day, you are the jerk.

Here's the thing, though: Emotions are not hard-wired, uncontrollable brain reactions. Nor are they genetically or socially preconditioned from birth. They are not permanent.

Emotions are built, crafted by our own limited experience. Our brains are often processing through memories, just trying to identify what event in the past the current one resembles—that rapid comparison of present and past influences how we see what is happening in front of us. We are relating scenes, people, and emotions, making predictions for where everything will go this time. When we are in a state of fear, we are usually afraid of something we have already survived, not a new experience. We exaggerate possibilities in our minds, but they are not foreign. We have been there before. Fearful forecasting is a bizarre and fascinating tendency to ponder. Even the emotions we see in other people are predictions based more on our own experiences from the past, not theirs. A mind racing through possibilities is nothing more than a search for a reasonable prediction to explain our sensations.

Our state affects how we receive and interpret information. It affects what we see, hear, feel, and even what we smell and taste. Fortunately, we are not at the mercy of the ancient reptilian or monkey brain. We have control over our emotions and moods. We must have an extensive catalog of positive emotions and experiences to draw from, as well. If we can change the ingredients and widen our range of emotional possibilities, we have better options to improve the outcomes. We must un-train ourselves from using our limited options from the past so the present can be better. Training our minds to have better options now also helps prepare us for tough times later. The necessary excavation concerning deeper psychology will come soon. For now, it's all about breaking patterns. Let's file this section under neurology and keep moving.

Attention and discipline, regarding where we focus, pay huge dividends. We must be mindful, attentive, and awake. If not sober and vigilant, the old program runs automatically, and we are once again just pawns in the already established game. An angry state makes many situations worse; a sad state can make some lousy things remain unchanged, and a hopeful state might make events a little better. Another person can recognize when our physiology is off and help us be accountable for improving it. But our internal focus often remains hidden, even to ourselves. We must learn to self-police those invisible parts of our nature. The untrained mind is reckless and dangerous. The average person has over 30,000 thoughts every day. If unmonitored and unregulated, these thoughts can create illness. We make ourselves sick with how we think. I had been doing this for years before realizing that I had options to change it all.

Fearful thoughts trigger hundreds of physical and chemical reactions in the body. Fear alone can activate a cascade of responses and stress hormones, even if the threat is only in our mind. In stark contrast, gratitude decreases cortisol levels and increases our problem-solving abilities. When we focus on gratitude, our brain releases neurotransmitters that rapidly boost our mood. Simple thoughts can influence our entire system. Gratitude is a curiously powerful emotion. An incredible thing to understand is that our brains cannot process gratitude and anxiety at the same time. In other words, you cannot be grateful and angry at the same time, or grateful and fearful at the same time. If you focus on one, the other ceases. They require different areas of the brain to process and are mutually exclusive. They can alternate but not function simultaneously.

I've heard many teachers advise people to write a list of things or people they are grateful for, which is probably not bad advice. But I have found that making a list was a little boring. And honestly, how many times can you do that and expect the same emotional results? Instead of making a list, I like to pick one item that I can express gratitude for and focus on that single thing for a while. That could be for two minutes or forty-five. After I finish that exercise, I often pick an additional item and sit with that one for a while. Some people may reflect on the same few things each day, but for me, there is always new material. The variety also fits well with my temperament.

Another thing I have become especially fond of is to replay a favorite event in my mind. That experience could be a significant accomplishment I was proud of, a time when I felt extreme love or belonging, or an event that caused me to laugh my tail off. It could be something intensely emotional, like watching the birth of a child. Or it could be something vain and pleasurable, like a favorite intimate experience.

Maybe for you, it's an exhilarating adventure that needs revisiting. Whatever it is, close your eyes and go there. Experience it again in your mind and relive the moments. The scenery, the faces, the smells, the emotions, soak it all in. Don't be in a hurry, enjoy it. It's incredible what emotions can be triggered and how dramatically the state can change in these exercises. I highly recommend it. It's shockingly simple and profoundly impactful, but again, it takes practice to become proficient. Get lost in one of your awesome memories and permit yourself to stay awhile to enjoy it.

Powerful Practice

Knowing that changing our physiology and our focus can rescue us from a sub-optimal state, we naturally have to ask the next question. What if we preemptively start and then continually intersperse the day with powerful posture, deliberate movement, and mindful thinking? Well, what would you expect to happen? There is no point in me going on about what you already intuitively suspect is true. The best thing you could do now is to try to prove me wrong. Test the tools and methods laid out in front of you. I first used these state change skills solely for rescue, when I realized I was in trouble. I now use them for prevention. These skills have enabled me to extinguish fires and also to prevent many more from ever starting. Besides perceived emotional benefits, my lab reports from blood and urinalysis freakishly improved after dutifully maintaining these techniques for a few weeks. Out of the hundreds of supplements, practices, exercises, and habits I have tested over the years, the practice of state management seems to be one of the most valuable methods to improve the human condition.

In time, we can arrive at a peaceful place where there aren't as many decisions to be made about where to focus. We stop wasting time and energy on unproductive actions. As the old patterns break and new ones get established, the automatic path becomes one that requires less thinking and less struggle. We learn to avoid damaging thoughts and emotions altogether, instead of needing a rescue. Our minds learn to stay on track and stick with more useful, more straightforward actions. It is in this place of balance and maturity that we learn how to do less and to be more.

It's important to refrain from making big decisions in a poor state. Try to move into a healthier place first. I'm learning, over and over, that when I'm angry, I should take no immediate action. It's too dangerous and can be the catalyst that starts a cascade of irreversible, potentially life-changing events. When I'm sad, I rarely see things accurately. When I'm tired, I take the lazy approach. When impatient, I choose what is expedient instead of what is wise. Many details get exaggerated in a poor state, and many others get overlooked.

I have also learned that most any decision made in a state of fear is the wrong one. It impedes our judgment and preys on us in times of weakness and instability. It is an evil force that can cripple us with harmful thoughts and emotions running amok. It causes us to exaggerate the dangers we face. Remember, darkness is present only in the absence of light. Whether literal, emotional, metaphorical, or spiritual, it is necessary to turn on the light to drive out the darkness. Fear need not have any place of prominence in our lives. We must chase it away as soon as we recognize it has encroached into our spaces.

You now have a niche knowledge that will change your life, once situation at a time. This isn't complicated. Recognize when you are in a state that does not align with optimal health and happiness and does not contribute to accomplishing your goals. Take action quickly to change your state before you overthink it or change your mind. Use both your body and your mind to escape. Change your physiology first, and then your focus. Do this as often as necessary until they become habitual and part of your identity.

The goal is simple: We are striving to become more self-aware, disciplined individuals. If we can learn to navigate our emotions, both the constructive and destructive ones, we will be able to achieve a higher level of success and happiness. Physiology and focus are your allies and no longer your adversaries. Using the body and mind instead of allowing it to use you changes everything. Knowing how to break a pattern is a powerful weapon to have in your arsenal. Wield it well and use it often.

CHAPTER 7
Getting Real with Yourself – Mindset

L EARNING HOW TO manage your state, break patterns, and create new habits is powerful. The active, two-stage process defined in the previous chapter is a dynamic weapon in well-trained hands. But without elevating our mental capacity, there is a ceiling on what we can do with it. The goal is to eventually arrive at a less volatile, more predictable place. At some point, we can demand less muscle and employ more wit. You can only get away with burpees in the boardroom so many times. We've raised the standards for our bodies. Now let's do the same for our thinking.

Do you know someone who gracefully goes with the flow and seamlessly adapts to life? Some extraordinary people seem to keep their cool at all times. They avoid getting derailed by unexpected events and miraculously do so in the absence of flippant emotions or any sense of entitlement. How do these people, so peacefully grounded and resolute, do it? Were they born that way, or did they make a critical decision to live differently? Could someone without the genetic predisposition for such a temperament cultivate it?

I always admired the peaceful, self-controlled types, but could never fully relate. I assumed those cool, calm, and collected people were operating on a different platform, one unavailable to me. I thought they must either be blissfully ignorant, extremely wise, smoking something, or just genetically built for permanently low blood pressure. I believed that I had too much energy to be so subdued. I had too many opinions to opt-out of conversations. I admired when people were right and could quietly allow the other person to be wrong, without needing to prove anything. I respected the people that could let things go. I never thought I could operate that way.

Somewhere amongst a pile of great books, a perplexing but simple question swirled into my thought tornado. It repeated:

What if you're wrong?

Once I started entertaining that vague, baseline question, many more piled up.

- *What if you are wrong about your own story, about who you are, about who you can be?*
- *What if you are wrong about the people around you?*
- *What if you are wrong about what's possible, about what you know, about everything?*
- *How many beliefs in your mind were implanted there by other people, outside influence, or limited experiences?*
- *How many of the events of your life have been embellished or warped over time?*
- *How many things do you do, believe, hear, and say because of patterns established from when you were more ignorant and insecure?*
- *Could all of this be changed?*
- *Could you develop a fresh mindset and a different temperament?*

Pondering better questions, I committed to hunt down a new phase of life, intentionally seeking more peace. It was time to develop a new character, or at least to evolve into a better one. Being willing to be wrong and courageous enough to look into painful places was an adequate starting place.

Becoming more open-minded became more comfortable as I reflected on just how stupid I was a few years back. I knew that a few years from now, I would feel that same way about today. If we are growing, we can look back and see how childish, unloving, selfish, arrogant, or inexperienced we were. It should be gratifying, not shameful, to look back and see foolishness. It validates growth and progress.

Character Rules

The linchpin in this grand plan of forming a superior mindset is the ability to choose the correct identity. We cannot aimlessly roam and expect major progress. We must select prudent and virtuous targets that fit within our desired character. Once we establish the specific goals for our being, everything starts orienting towards them. It may be useful to focus on a single item at a time. If I decide that I will craft my character around endurance, I now have a clear mission. Now, everything in life is about pacing, finishing the race, pushing through, and not giving up. If I choose peace as my identity, all of my actions center toward that waypoint. I can now disengage from futile spats, choose reconciliation over vindication, be a conscientious mediator for opposing groups, or be able to walk away from foolish engagements. If I choose to be love, all of my decisions begin to pass through a filter where ego-driven selfishness has a chance to be removed, and actions can be crafted based on the good of others.

Once we focus on a single positive thing, we begin to see opportunities for it everywhere. Unfortunately, the opposite is true too. If all we are looking for is something negative, we will find it, even if we have to distort the story. We modify details to match our intention. Multiple witnesses will recount the exact same event with different details based on the mindset of the viewer. A politician's speech will be interpreted based on the listener's attitude, not the speaker's words or intent.

We combat our natural tendencies for stress and anxiety when we learn to let go. We must loosen our grip on the things we can't control and tightly grasp onto the few things that we can. We must first be a sage, letting go of the foolish sentiments, before suiting up as a soldier to fight. Otherwise, we engage in too many battles and sustain unnecessary injuries. At some point, there comes a need to surrender so many of our thoughts, actions, and relationships. These longstanding ideas have become our friends, addictions, and our masters. But after proper evaluation and clarity, we know we must turn thoughts loose and turn a new direction. They have served us for a long time, meeting our needs in ways that may no longer be acceptable. We are too good to keep the old patterns. Many of them have become a waste of time and a detriment to our character. If we do not cleave from the things that are making us sick, we will be further damaged. We must learn to surrender to increase our faith. The surrender serves to vanquish our fears. Some people may surrender them back to fate. Others may give them to God. Many consider those the same thing.

There are many rules we expect other people to follow. But instead of demanding that they change their behaviors, we should establish our rules and stick to our own covenants. When we do, we have a chance to settle down and demand less of the world. It's not complicated. We already know some of the rules, because our expectations impose them on everyone else:

Be polite. Smile. Don't lie. Take turns. Help each other. Share. Play fairly. Keep your cool. Be patient. Don't steal. Be merciful. Do no harm. Be a team player. Don't overreact. Work hard. Pull your weight. Stop complaining. Clean up after yourself. Don't spend more money than you make. Don't hate. Don't gossip. Don't be nosy. Respect people's space.

But why is it necessary to develop a superior mindset and

character? Why not just be an impulsive, hedonistic narcissist? No, really, why not?

Inner Conflict

The word hypocrite comes from the Greek word for an actor. When we tout one identity but live another, we remain in conflict with ourselves. Depression and anxiety plague us when we see ourselves acting in contrast to our values. This phenomenon is also known as guilt. We have inner turmoil because we know we are wasting, hiding, and failing. We are doing things we know we should not do and failing to do things we know we should do. We are letting people down, both ourselves and others. Even if we're unconscious of the emotions, they affect us. We misdirect our anger and frustration, shoveling it onto other people and problems, but the root issue is guilt. Guilt is more insidious and more far-reaching than we prefer to admit.

When we are falling short, we craft stories to mask our inconsistencies. However, they don't produce any lasting peace, only chaos. Eventually, we get called on our bluff. Then we make more excuses and point fingers to ease our guilt. Justifying our shortcomings and pretending we don't see them is a terrible surrogate for real action and virtue. I can blame my workplace, my spouse, my kids, my lack of support, or even my DNA for my problems, but to what avail? The problem is still sitting there, unresolved. When I'm willing to accept an excuse in place of the goal itself, I should admit that I never wanted it badly enough in the first place. My actions expose my true passions, or lack thereof. They are condemning. We can often fool others, but not ourselves.

At times, we totally ignore the shortcomings in our virtue or pretend they don't matter. Other times we acknowledge the importance of virtue but refuse concrete action. We claim to be an advocate for the planet, but we fail to make inconvenient adjustments to help remedy the problem. Instead, we point fingers and protest big industrial polluters while making no effort to live a more sustainable lifestyle. We talk about the desire for organizing, eliminating debt, spending more time with family, or becoming more active in the community, but our actions don't match the rhetoric.

Have you ever noticed that we pretend that voicing a problem is the same thing as fixing it? Why would I need to say, "I shouldn't eat this cupcake" just before I stuff it into my mouth? It doesn't make me sound intelligent. It only highlights my lack of discipline. It's like we want everyone else to know that we are aware that what we are doing is foolish. What a strange but very normal tendency. That reminds me, I should go to the gym today and get back into church.

Being honest is more freeing than seeming virtuous. Instead of saying, "If I had your schedule, I would work-out every day too," or "If I had your money, I would donate too," we should admit that those things are not as important to us as the things we are doing in their place. We go after what we want, whether healthy or not. We also lie about what we truly want.

So, what does your conscience say needs attention? What does it say is wrong with the current picture? What are you anxious, sad, or angry about? Those answers can reveal a place for action. We must either change our interpretation of the problem or take action to dissolve it. Do we make essential adjustments to fight the issues that plague us multiple times per day? Or do we remain unchanged, all while resenting the boss, coworkers, family members, and other people who aren't living the way we desire? Are we victims, maintaining the problem because it gives us a permanent excuse for so many other issues? After all, if work is too demanding, we not only lack time for our family, but also for religion, charity, play, or self-care. There are so many cop-outs on the ready. "I can't cook real food because I am too busy. My only option is fast food because I am so chained down. I'll fix it when I get rich." Are you a person who fixes things, or one who is abused by them? You cannot be both.

I realize that much of this sounds uncharitable or hyperbolic, but I am speaking from experience. When I realized that I needed to spend more time with my family, it required real sacrifice and much more intense work. It wasn't fun or easy to make the necessary adjustments. It would have been much more comfortable short-term to leave it unchanged, but the long-term cost was too great to ignore the call.

Specifying a problem is unpleasant because when it's right in our line of sight, we are forced to contend with it. Sometimes we would rather pretend to be blind than to admit something is glaring us in the face. We must be willing to assess where we are and grade it against where we know we should be. That introspection is difficult. It takes courage because we know it will demand of us. Seeing that our actions conflict with our values is condemning. Knowing this principle, we need a mindset that encourages progress instead of hiding from it.

Mindset

When we have a healthier mindset, oriented toward individual responsibility and character, the world around us is a different place. In the absence of angst and guilt, we can develop the capacity to become more calculated and less impulsive. We are less threatened by trivial things, and more concerned with things that matter. Not only do we become comfortable being wrong, we no longer have a need to be right. We can remove our biases and see more truth. Whether or not we agree with someone else, it shouldn't matter. It does not affect our mission or identity. If it remains unchecked, our dualistic thinking automatically draws lines and forms alliances. We naturally want to build walls, classify ideas and people, and separate them into groups. This way of thinking is lazy and requires less effort. If we can't cultivate a compassionate understanding of human nature, tribalism is the default, and we take sides. Without a mature balance and wisdom, we force things to be black or white, right or wrong, gay or straight, republican or democrat, Jew or gentile, etc. We search for convenient, either/or answers instead of considering both/and options.

An all-or-nothing approach is usually a recipe for gridlock and tribal warfare. To be at peace with other groups, we should be able to sympathize, have discussions, and listen. This is particularly difficult when we are in self turmoil or are wounded and hurting. Everyone is partially right, partially wrong, and somewhat justified in what they think. The same goes for you and me.

To be innocent in any matter, we must return to the original Latin definition of the word, which means "not hurt." To have a chance to grow, we must step into a different mindset. We have to learn how to be unwounded, and also learn how to stop wounding others. That requires some maturation, transcending problems, and forgiveness. That F-word is serious business and often extremely hard to pull off. It is counter-cultural to be unwounded and to refuse to be a victim. It has somehow become socially acceptable to be wound-identified and to have an existence based on that wound. It's a source of sympathy and too often an excuse for not becoming an adult. Wounding others is a quick way to feel better about ourselves, but recklessly selfish. We tear others down to make ourselves look better. After all, the fastest way to have the tallest building in town is to burn down all the other buildings. But acting like a terrorist is in direct opposition to our values, so once again, we lose.

The goal should be to remain humble, which is a mindset where we can be grateful for experiencing life and where no one owes us anything. As Mother Teresa of Calcutta put it, "If you are humble, nothing will touch you; neither praise nor disgrace, because you know what you are."

That quote begs the question; What are we?

You can answer that for yourself, and you should. For me, the answer goes something like this:

You are fallible but good.

You are wounded but not maimed.

You are competent but dangerous.

You are greedy with the potential for compassion.

You are a lover with the capacity for hatred.

You are valuable but replaceable.

You are a cowardly hero, a wealthy beggar, and a faithful doubter.

You are intelligently uneducated and a capable novice.

Aiming for innocence, we set the bar extremely high, but that's what is required to experience peace. We may never fully arrive, but without a target destination, we will always choose the easy way out.

Better Questions / Better Answers

Motivation can be created, but thankfully, it also descends upon us unexpectedly sometimes. A fundamental problem many of us have is that when we have a moment of strength and energy, we misdirect it. The opportunity is wasted because we are either asleep, lacking a concrete plan, or are looking for the wrong thing. We ask the wrong questions, which produce the wrong actions, or none at all. We ask:

What should I do now?

Where should I run?

What sweeping solution will save me from this mediocrity?

What can I purchase to supplement success?

What could I add to make things move faster?

We fantasize about new relationships, new environments, or new activities that will fix everything in one fell swoop. We wait for the voice of God, serendipity, or genius to strike and give us a sign for the next major directive that will lead to salvation. But when we don't have a favorable answer, we too often do nothing.

Instead of asking what I *should* do, I decided a better strategy was to listen to my inner voice telling me what I definitively *should not* do. There is always a list for that. We rarely prefer to obey this voice, but it speaks all the time. It often speaks the language of anxiety, depression, lethargy, or anger. It doesn't sound like the romantic hero were are listening for, so we often miss the messages. While waiting for an optimal and painless path to manifest, we absent-mindedly continue strolling down the trail covered in snakes and thorns. Sometimes we are waiting for a perfect option, instead of choosing one that is at least a bit better. We may not know which way to go, but we do know where we shouldn't stay.

It may not totally save my marriage, but deciding to stop yelling disrespectfully is something. It may not make me lose 70 pounds, but placing a moratorium on fast food will certainly help. Maybe my plight won't be totally rectified, but I could stop buying liquor, quit browsing social media, or stop booking trips to the casino. Simply deciding to avoid environments that encourage or allow poor states and harmful behaviors is huge progress. We could avoid certain areas of town, the office, the grocery store, or even the internet. The ultimate solution we are dreaming of to create harmony and happiness may not even exist. That dream may be just another childish distraction to avoid doing hard work.

What determines what we should and should not do? We have to acknowledge that we possess some ideology that determines our hierarchy of values. We have some personal ideas of what we regard as virtuous, respectable, or necessary to live well. We hold many other people to these standards of virtue and moral codes, but give ourselves a pass too often. We need to define what is expected and permissible behavior, and what is not.

Think about living without guilt. What would it be like to know you are satisfied with your work? How would it feel to know you are offering your best, continually improving? What sort of state would you live in if you knew you could look into the mirror, into the eyes of a loved one, or even in the face of God, and know you are doing your part? We cannot fool ourselves for long or lie to ourselves about the work. We must do it. Blame and excuses are not a sustainable solution. We have to be the person we know we should be to create the freedom we desire.

We are emotional creatures by design. The goal is not to abolish emotions. Rather, we must guard them, knowing how quickly things spiral out of control when we don't. When threatened or wounded, we are capable of corruption. We must strive to live in a state where we stay appropriately nourished and less needy. If somehow, we can adopt the proper mindset, we can avoid much of the typical drama and chaos that wrecks everyday life. I hesitate to use the word untouchable, but with the right mindset, we can at least be much more resistant to the troubles of the common world. We can operate outside of the standard model of emotions. As Marcus Aurelius states, "Choose not to be harmed, and you won't feel harmed. If you don't feel harmed, you haven't been." When we enter this realm of thinking, many of the people around us cannot comprehend our actions or lack thereof. That's fine because being understood is no longer required in our new model.

What determines whether or not we will take on necessary actions? There must be an exhaustive list of possibilities, but I want to highlight two elements that I have learned to keep in question: desire and courage.

Desire

What we desire at any given moment shapes our perception of everything that happens around us. Desire influences our vision, but it is also a product of vision. We see a limited range of obstacles and remedies based on what we have learned to focus upon. We look at what we want to look at and only see what we want to see. Desire arises from the necessities of life, but necessities are relative, and they change over time. How do we assure that we want the correct things? This is where moral and character boundaries come into play. We must check our desires against our goals of virtue.

How do we cultivate desire? Many people will only do something challenging when the risk of not doing it is higher than the pain of doing it. Remaining stagnant shows that something is not important to us, or at least not important enough to move. When we know what is necessary, but cannot do it, our desire must be questioned. It's possible that that thing is not very important and can be dismissed from our obsessive thinking. But often, it is worthwhile, and we have not fully considered the risks and benefits of both outcomes. Asking what the pain will be next year, in five years, or ten, if we remain unchanged and do nothing, is a worthy exercise. When I notice I lack motivation or desire for something I know I need to do, I write out two scenarios. One list is how my lazy and selfish inactions will affect life later. The other list is how my disciplined actions would affect the future if I execute them well. Who will win and lose from my decision today? Not reigning in finances, weight gain, or communication problems with your partner carries major costs. The longer we wait, the harder the recovery. The only better time than today to start getting serious was yesterday

To prevent anxiety and depression, we have to orient ourselves toward our highest goals of virtue and character. We must decide what we want our mindset to be and then put in the work. Hiding creates chaos and displaces order. Emotions should not trump intellect. Fear should not stifle noble action.

Do you want to reconcile with your father, to lose weight, or to get out of debt? Or do you like to pretend that you are trying? Do you want it bad enough to do it? Have you considered what happens if you don't attempt to repair the damage? Have you thought about how many things flourish when the issues have been resolved?

We like to blame a lack of resources for our stagnancy, but the thing we are lacking is resourcefulness. We do what we want to do. If we want it bad enough, we will find a way. When we will not move, we must be honest and admit that our desire is probably lacking. If unwilling to work, we should reevaluate our desire.

Courage - Faith & Fear

There's an influential dichotomy affecting our courage at all times. The interplay between faith and fear is something we should ponder. We cannot see some things or believe in them if we lack faith. We cannot see others because of the presence of fear. Faith gives us the assurance that some things are worth doing. Fear is constantly attacking those beliefs, pestering us to reconsider.

Faith and fear are both natural. Fear grows automatically, but fortifying our faith takes prudent effort. We can build confidence in ourselves, God, other people, or systems. Our unique combination of faith and fear determines how we see the past, present, and future. Interestingly, one grows as the other withers, like weeds in a garden. Robust weeds choke out the desirable plants. In contrast, thriving crops can block out the unwanted weeds, starving them off and possibly killing them.

Perhaps the best way to cultivate faith is to eradicate fear. If we continuously remove the weeds and wait for sunlight and rain, the good stuff should eventually grow. We can at least develop territory where it has the resources needed to mature. The yin and yang blend of chaos and order will always be present in our lives and constantly changing. We cannot expect to avoid turmoil and pain but should maintain some level of control over the proportional mix. Prepare fertile soil and keep pulling weeds. Eradicate fear to create space for confidence and faith.

It's laborious to manufacture faith from our limited wisdom, morality, courage, and moderation. But we can, at a minimum, refrain from folly, start telling the truth, stop entertaining oppressive fears, and pull back on our immature behaviors. These seemingly simple actions are far from insignif-icant. Our faith and security in virtue build as we remove the setbacks to them. We must deliberately and tirelessly choose the best option, or at a minimum, the less evil one.

For me, fear seemed to be enemy number one, inhibiting my quest for peace. Fear is such an insidious thing that creeps into every aspect of life when we aren't soberly watchful. I thought ego was to blame for a while because so much pain and anxiety come from pride. But ego is only actively volatile in the presence of some fear. Anger, jealousy, control, rejection, resentment, anxiety, stress, and so many other sentiments that plague us are the first cousins of fear, if not just fear with other names. Before making any efforts to make my identity about love, I had to take a smaller step first and orient my identity toward courage. Courage is doing what we must do despite the fear. This requires a level of vulnerability. Over time, if we remain devoted to courage, fear subsides. When fear dissipates, we can respond differently to life because we are no longer so threatened. Then we can see more clearly what we should be doing.

Embracing Reality

At some point, maybe we can stop fighting life and roll with it, developing *amor fati*, a Latin phrase translated as "love of one's fate." It describes an attitude in which one sees everything that happens in life, including pain and loss, as good, or at least necessary. In this mindset, we can accept the events of life, and possibly see them as opportunities. We certainly prefer to avoid suffering, but when it finds us, we accept that it's our turn and try to push through gracefully. We cannot avoid it, and grumbling about it doesn't help. How we suffer matters, and there are many options for how to do it.

Surrender is not the same thing as defeat. There are times when we should take up arms and fight. But many battles we engage in are futile, resulting from our pain, insecurity, or inability to sit still. The proper mindset is not only a surrender of many intense emotions and opinions, but also a change in expectations. Friedrich Nietzsche discussed the concept of "eternal recurrence" as the idea that with infinite time and a finite number of possible human events, some events are bound to recur. We should not be surprised or dismayed when we experience the tragedies of life that we have seen others go through. Life is a series of facts. Resisting facts or arguing against them does little good. Human fate shows patterns. We should not expect to avoid the ills of life.

Change is inevitable. Whether we regard it as exciting or terrifying does not change the onset, only the resolution. We can either seize opportunities for growth or cower in crippling fear. Some anxiety is useful because it grabs our attention and prompts action. We probably cannot avoid all the stress associated with change, but we can choose how we manage it. Two people waiting in line for the same roller coaster ride have similar brain chemistry, but different interpretations. One rider can be thrilled with the nervous energy, while the other is paralyzed with fear. One thinks of the worst, and the other focuses on the best. The same can go for many experiences, voluntary or not. Waiting for lab work to return from the doctor's office can be empowering or crushing, depending on our mindset. Asking someone out for a date could be our ticket out of loneliness or a guarantee of more heartbreak.

The way we frame an experience matters. Regarding the emotional outlook, it's disingenuous to say, "Just look on the bright side" or "Focus on the positive." A better option may be to evaluate whether there is any benefit to entertaining the anxiety. The high energy state could function as a reminder to be more calculated and cautious for one individual, and a reminder just to let loose for another. In general, that which does not disturb us is self-determined to be okay. The same event can have different meanings at different times. We interpret those things that trouble us as problems, even though they may be opportunities to grow. We must establish what we want, what we need, and what we will allow to bother us.

Beyond knowing what we are, it's imperative also to understand who we are. So many of us define what we are against but never establish what we stand for. Asking what you want people to remember you for is the wrong question. Being concerned with what other people see is the wrong focus. The better questions are: Who do you want to see when you look in the mirror, or better still, when you look inwardly? Who are you at your core? These questions are not dependent on anyone else. If no one ever sees, understands, or appreciates the process, you must still do the work to resolve and deter the inner conflict. We externalize so many problems and blame outside sources, but the root problem is likely individual, as is the solution. The true self begs for a resolution when our actions contradict our values.

Happiness or Peace

Happiness should not be the principal goal of a healthy mindset. There are too many times in life when we will not be happy. If happiness is the metric we track, we will fail. Being happy is a temporary gift and not sustainable. Life is full of unavoidable tragedy and devastation. Hardships will come. The goal of a healthy mindset should be peace. Even in the middle of tragedy and pain, there can still be peace. We begin to experience peace when we distance ourselves from our obsessions and stay focused on who we need to be.

Several years ago, I found myself in a living hell. I was getting my tail kicked as a father, trying to figure out how to raise a child with special needs. I felt like I was failing the most significant role in my life. After back-to-back miscarriages and the indescribable pain that comes from watching the person you love most endure such suffering, another baby finally arrived. He was supposed to be our saving grace, but he arrived extremely sick. I knew how to deal with losing a child in the womb, but I did not know how to deal with having a child that could not breathe on his own, who was just diagnosed with severe brain damage. I did not know how to minister to a mother who had gracefully endured so much and needed me to be something more than tired, afraid, and depressed.

I reached out to my older, wiser brother for counsel. He is a man of extreme faith and truth. I'll never forget what he told me. He reminded me that no one escapes suffering or should expect to do so. He said, "God never promises us we can avoid suffering. He promises that we will suffer, but that we will never be abandoned in it." Then he gave me a little hard-nosed advice that has stayed with me ever since. He challenged me as a man and told me to keep showing up. He said, "When you wake up in the morning, all you can do is put your two feet on the floor and give it all you've got. Your vocation as a husband and a father never changes. Your calling is the same every day. Keep showing up and doing your job." He went on to say that no matter what the situation or season, I was called to the same thing every day. That calling was to give everything I had to this family, even if some days there was very little to give. It is in that process that I could somehow find peace. You will have no chance of rest with your head on the pillow if you know you didn't do the work that day. No one can expect more of you if you have honestly done your best. You can clock in, give it all you have, then clock out, and surrender it to God.

I am grateful that my loving brother did not say, "Everything is going to be OK" or "It could be worse." Instead, he affirmed that my situation sucked and that I was capable of what was being asked of me. He reminded me that whether my son passed away that night or was permanently disabled for life, my individual responsibilities would never change. He encouraged me to keep punching my timecard every day and doing the work. Courage and persistence were the only viable choices. Those were the things that would prevent looking back with disdain for myself if I chose poorly. So instead of staying depressed and continuing to get pounded, I got back on offense. I showed up and did what I needed to do. I maintained my attitude, posture, faith, support, love, prayers, appreciation, endurance, and love the best that I knew how.

In a fortunate chain of events that could only be described as miraculous, my son fully recovered. The doctor had nothing else to say about the harrowing MRI images or his prior diagnosis. While we were at our worst, a loving community rallied around us, offering compassionate thoughts, prayers, and actions for my family. After ten days of emergency care and quarantined monitoring, we were dismissed to go home with no further issues. If you are curious as to whether prayer changes medical outcomes, look up the peer-reviewed studies published on it. A few are quite interesting.

Speaking of prayer and miracles, It's now appropriate to insert an additional mindset issue. Everyone has some form of religion. That is a set of rules, beliefs, and structures that govern how we think and act. Children, pets, and adults function better in a system with some regulations, expectations, and boundaries. We must operate within them for a while to understand where limits are and where we should push. Struggling with the rules may be necessary before trying to reformulate them. We should conservatively learn to walk on a leash before being allowed to roam liberally. Everyone has some foundation or system for morality. There may be no such thing as living areligious. I say this because there seem to be staunch, dividing lines around people's beliefs, based on their group identities. We are only comfortable discussing another religious ideology or philosophy once we are somewhat content with our own. Our level of assumptions, judgment, and tolerance of others determines whether we can have civil discourse. Much of our disgust and anger with other parties is a manifestation of our guilt, struggling with our own system of rules. Unfortunately, we do not always see the world as it is. We see the world as we are, which is why we need mindset standards. Spiritual health and emotional health are probably not separable. They are a package deal and only possible when we are honestly living within the boundaries that we know are true and beautiful.

If I may push it one step further with religious language, everyone has idols. These are probably not deities per se, but objects and ideas. We worship something, whether it's notoriety, power, wealth, sex, intelligence, or something else. We all need work. We should concern ourselves with living our best life, not feuding with everyone else who we self-determine is not.

We must first remove the plank from our own eye before we can help remove the splinter from someone else's. It's not our job to fix everyone. It's our job to keep fixing ourselves. What we give largely determines what we get back. It's a strange law of the universe. That goes for kindness and tact, or unfairness and vitriol. Attitudes circle back.

We should listen more and speak less. Even if you love your platform and want others to join you there, people will not come without a very compelling reason. That reason would be an example of someone who is living an attractive, fruitful life. Like a wise man once told me after we witnessed a heated theological debate, "No one comes to Jesus because they lost an argument." Intolerant rage is not attracting anyone to your point of view, nor is it assisting your journey. Before people are willing to come to your school of thinking, they will need to see a compelling and beautiful life.

The Greatest Teacher

An additional item to consider when pondering how to craft the best mindset is how to view failure. We cringe from the thought of failure, until hopefully one day, it becomes a dear friend and teacher. We must have the courage to come up short, knowing that failure is often the best way to grow. We learn how to fall by repeatedly falling. I do not mean we should be brave enough to consider failure. Rather, we should be brave enough to fail. We should expect it and maybe even learn to celebrate it. If you are willing to step into the arena for any length of time, you will lose matches. You will probably sustain injuries along the way. They are part of the process. No one is entitled to circumvent failure, rejection, or shame. We can only change what they mean to us and how we respond to them. If we fail, we should decipher where things went off the rails, then reset, shake it off, and start again tomorrow. If we aren't failing, we are probably either not pushing hard enough, or not being honest in our self- evaluation.

The Power of Your Word

A strategic component of this mindset shift is to appreciate the immense power of our language. We must make a deliberate decision to strive to be impeccable in our word. This is certainly easier said than done. Words and thoughts are powerful weapons. They change lives for better or worse, in our own life, and the lives of others. We must stop speaking too quickly, flippantly, or thoughtlessly. If there has been no thinking, there should be no words. If there has been little thought, but only in a poor state, there should still be no words. Opinions influence outcomes. So before broadcasting our views, we should carefully discern them.

We must consider how we send information, but also how we receive it. Some of the things once spoken about you, without your permission, became unwritten agreements. The same goes for what we say about others. We see most every situation through the eyes of prior spoken words. This can even happen internally. We speak to ourselves so disrespectfully sometimes. Words can stoke fires or extinguish them. They can build people up or tear them down. Use the tongue as a medical device, not a weapon. We should strive to be careful in our speech and learn to refrain from speaking foolishly or inaccurately.

We should maintain the utmost respect for the gravity of words. What we speak about a situation has a much higher probability of becoming a reality that what is not. This is true whether the statements are positive or negative. Many teachers and parents will reinforce that a child is a hyperactive discipline problem, but who benefits from the audible comment? Does that help the child improve, or does it make the adults feel better about the struggle? Does anything need to be said at all? Could you offer something more constructive and useful?

Forty-year-old women still vividly remember life-altering comments from the seventh grade. One poorly calculated response from a heated spouse can affect relationships for decades. A degrading or absent-minded remark from a dad can destroy a personality. Even a banal comment about something insignificant can start a cascade of lifelong emotional responses. The same thing happens with comments from a supervisor, a friend, or a stranger. Be impeccable in your speech and appreciate that so many others are not.

We are hurt by the words of others, and we hurt people with our own. We are simultaneously the oppressor and the oppressed. The question is, do you still need to be either one? There is a solution. The contrarian mindset of the emotionally stable involves a considerable capacity for forgiveness. The greatest gift we can give ourselves is the ability to forgive. It is a developed skill. Whether it's a parent, a family member, friends, legitimate enemies, fictional enemies, strangers, or even God, it is imperative to be able to forgive. Unforgiveness is a raging infection, a malignant disease. It violently spreads into every aspect of our being. It destroys our true selves. Even if those around you don't deserve your forgiveness, you deserve it. You are the one who benefits the most from practicing the act of mercy. An old familiar saying states that harboring unforgiveness and resentment is like drinking poison but expecting the other person to die.

When we are un-wounded, even for a brief moment, we can see people differently. We can see their suffering and offer our best selves through pardoning and forgiveness. That opportunity is a grace. We can give someone the mercy that they do not deserve when we recognize that it's such a winning proposition. We will need it again in time, and so will they. It is more than just careful thoughts or words. Forgiving actually changes us in our core. One day, after many repetitions, we can hear the name of our oppressor and not be triggered. We can view them as a wounded child, without contempt, malice, or anxiety. We are immune to their attacks and possibly even compassionate toward their plight.

Hope for the Best and Plan for the Worst

Once we are clear in what we intend to be, we can set ourselves up for better success. When we are at our best, we should be dutifully training for the worst. Nothing lasts forever, and seasons change. The sun may be out now, but another storm will manifest soon enough. Lucius Seneca wrote, "It is in times of security that the spirit should be preparing itself to deal with difficult times; while fortune is bestowing favors on it then is the time for it to be strengthened against her rebuffs." For thousands of years, religions and philosophies have encouraged followers to practice poverty voluntarily. Perhaps this exercise reminds us of how fragile we are. It connects us to the more profound awareness of the suffering of others and cultivates more compassion. It potentially makes us more grateful for our privileges. But possibly, it's just a form of dress rehearsal so that when we find ourselves in an otherwise desperate situation, we already know what to do.

My preferred method to prepare for pending trouble is to run through likely scenarios and preemptively plan responses to them. Prepare to keep your wits. Before taking a family vacation, I mentally prepare for less than ideal situations and rehearse them in my head. There is no need to have ongoing anxiety about all the details, but it is useful to consider the emotional possibilities if things go awry.

What should my temperament be if the flight is canceled or the bags get lost?

How will I respond to family members on this trip if situations or discussions get dicey?

What attitude will I carry if provoked?

How will I react to business emergencies that may arise while I am away?

These seem trivial, but something as simple as an unexpected long wait for dinner, a lost wallet, or a small fender bender could legitimately ruin a vacation if we are mentally unprepared. Planning to have the proper mindset may be the best form of trip insurance.

At the risk of sounding very strange, I'm going to take it a step further. Before entering a potentially stressful situation, I've learned to select the archetype character that I need to adopt for the duration. When I speak in front of a large crowd that terrifies me, I can tap into the archetype of the warrior. He is an alter ego that is more courageous than my typical self. If I know I will be around people that may challenge, provoke, or disrespect me, I invoke the inner character of the sovereign king. He's an old sage that has seen it all and done it all. The king is a wise leader, unharmed by reckless words, impervious to invitations for senseless fighting or petty arguments. At other times I could choose to be the magician or jester who can remain detached, unprovoked, and have a good time maintaining a playful sense of humor. In another case, the lover may be the best archetypal choice, seeing the purest part of everyone else and keeping their needs ahead of my own. If I don't premeditate these characters, I am more likely to mess things up. These are not fictional characters. They are parts of my being and of yours too.

When I choose to focus on myself and avoid seeing other's pain, I behave differently than when I pre-plan a higher purpose. After repeatedly practicing these characters over time, they slowly become more welded into permanency. Mindset leads to character change. We must choose to develop the right mindset because the default setting is too dangerous. A non-contemplative mind produces much unnecessary pain and delays maturation.

Unfavorable seasons will come, and we will survive them. But the next time one shows up, we should sustain fewer injuries than last time. We should also be able to help more people through it. We should not be anxious about a downturn, but dutifully training for it. Regardless of how weathered we feel, being the unshakeable rock in the storm is a fulfilling premise. People need someone to count on, and so do you. Someone else may have filled this role for you in the past. Now it's time for you to be the immovable foundation. There is real security in knowing that you are ready for the task. Even if we don't know all the required steps, we can rest easy knowing that we can handle ourselves.

Developing a superior mindset is not an overnight process. It could take years, if not decades. We must acknowledge this and grant some level of patience and grace, both to ourselves and to others. Comparing ourselves to others is a futile endeavor. There are too many variables to compare. We have different life experiences, opportunities, talents, biology, family, relationships, setbacks, education, and so much more. We are not comparable to anyone else. Everyone is on a different path but, hopefully, making progress in the right direction. Be merciful to others. Mind your own business. The only thing we should compare is where we are now and where we were last year.

Choosing Your Tribe

The final element in a decent mindset paradigm is establishing who gets to offer criticism and feedback about us.

121

People who say that they don't care what other people think of them are lying. We do care what people think, and often we should. We just need to be discriminating about who we allow to discriminate. In a world where everyone has an opinion and now has unlimited platforms to share it, sometimes anonymously, we must establish some reasonable parameters. We already established that comparison with others is futile, hazardous, and inaccurate. We only need to be compared with the best version of ourselves. We will never please everyone, so it's critical to establish some distance between non-credible sources of feedback.

We must have emotional boundaries. The people that we should listen to are the wiser people that live well, love us, and want the best for us. These should be people who desire to see us grow, and do not get threatened by the progress. This could be family, friends, or a hired professional. If we are closer and more vulnerable to people, they can hurt and punish us more easily. Don't take it personally. It's much less about you than you think.

Misery does love company, but luckily, so do peace and playfulness. Choose your friends wisely. Mindsets are contagious. There is some group out there, somewhere, willing to support any idea, no matter how ignorant or destructive it may be. When I choose rage, victimhood, or oppression, it's easy to find support for it. Remember that many "isms" of the world do not foster love and compassion. We will also find someone who is offended by any message, no matter how pious. If you are always the smartest person in the room, find a different room. Discover ways to foster relationships with elders. If everyone around you agrees on every issue, you're either in a stagnant culture or some sort of a cult. A group of people who look different but think the same is not diversity. We must remain challenged enough to seek answers, to be motivated for constant self-examination, and have opportunities to grow. We must learn to be content, both in times of plenty and in times of poverty. In either situation, we should apprentice under someone ahead of us, whether in person or through books. Friends are also seasonal in life as we grow, move, and change.

The refreshing thing about mindset changes is how rapidly they can occur. Once you take action on a particular thing, you are no longer someone who hasn't done that thing. If you jump out of a plane, you are no longer someone who would never skydive. Once you go on a weekend silent retreat, you are no longer someone who can't sit still with your mouth shut. (Use tape if you need to.)

Similarly, when we begin to think in new ways, we quickly become someone else. Mindset influences emotions. Emotions influence actions. Actions determine character. Choosing a superior way to see and interpret the world quickly contributes to the evolution of our best self. Most people never leave their comfort zone unless they are forced out. However, voluntarily leaving a former way of thinking, or at least welcoming a new way, is way less painful than being forcefully evicted through an unexpected disaster. Mindsets can automatically and easily drift in the wrong direction or dilute when we get complacent. It takes regular evaluation and re-centering, continually asking the hard questions. These require time for contemplation.

Let's craft a mindset that allows inevitable growth in multiple directions. Let's continually move towards an identity of supreme character and virtue. Let's loosen up a little, and maybe welcome the process of being wrong, failing, and being humbled by the facts of life. Let's embrace *amor fati* and start loving the journey. And while traveling, watch your mouth.

CHAPTER 8
Why We Do What We Do
– Human Needs

H UMAN PSYCHOLOGY CAN be perplexing, even intimidating, but understanding why we do what we do is paramount to becoming the best version of yourself. Hopefully, with some physiological changes in the bag, you feel ready to go deeper into new psychological territory. In studying numerous models of human behavior over the years, I stumbled over one that is profoundly practical, and I found it in a most unlikely place: in an arena blasting hip hop music for 10,000 screaming fans. Abraham Maslow was not in attendance, but some of his ideas indeed were.

The Invitation

One day while learning about Clare Graves and spiral dynamics online, a pop-up window appeared on my screen, advertising a four-day event in Los Angeles. I had consciously decided that on my quest to find a life with more peace and less anxiety, I would consider everything. So, I clicked the link and watched a video about this particular event. For decades, thousands of people attended this Tony Robbins' seminar, each paying $800 to $3000 for a seat. Many of the same people go back year after year, claiming that it permanently changed their lives. It's not an insignificant thing to produce $10 million in ticket sales for one weekend and not have rampant, post-purchase dissonance afterward. And while it was unnerving to picture myself in a foreign environment with a crowd of hyped-up, quasi-religious enthusiasts, I had to check it out. I clicked the link to buy my ticket for Unleash the Power Within before I could talk myself out of it. I could not think of anyone that would even consider going with me, but I decided to buy an additional ticket anyway and secured two spots.

A few weeks passed, and I couldn't convince anyone else to go. I was sitting in my meditation chair, considering whether I should sell the other ticket online. I prayed that whoever got the ticket for the now sold-out event would experience lasting growth from it. During that prayer, a chime sounded across the room. It was my closed laptop. I opened it to find a Facebook notification about a post from a teenage girl. I had never received a Facebook notification on my laptop before and had not been on the site in months. I recognized the girl in the photo. Her father was a beloved friend of mine that I enjoyed hanging out with before he moved out of state. I hadn't seen or spoken to him in over a year. I figured this must be a prompting to call him. I dialed him up, explained what happened, and invited him to travel with me to the event. He quickly informed me that he had no desire to go and couldn't afford the trip anyway. I told him the ticket, flight, and hotel were all covered, and that he should think about it for 24 hours and let me know then. He said he would call me back, but would not accept the invite or the act of charity. I told him that I wanted him to go because I loved him, not because I thought he needed fixing or because he was some sort of charity case.

Twenty-three and a half hours later, my phone rang. Before I could even finish saying hello, my friend said, "Damn it. I'm going." A month later, we headed to LA, having no idea what was in front of us. We decided that no matter how awkward or uncomfortable, we were going to be all-in. If the man said to jump, we would leap. If he told us to scream, we would do it with purpose. Little did we know that we would be repeatedly be asked to do both for 12 hours straight. And that was just on day one.

After the first day of high-energy education, introspection, exploration, and growth, we headed to the hotel exhausted. Before turning down for the night, my buddy began to weep. As he passed me his phone, he said, "I don't want to tell you about this, but I've got to. Just read it." I began to read the note on the screen. It was a suicide letter, addressed to his wife, whom he loved dearly. The next page was a letter to his daughter and the third one, a note to his son. It was one of the most grueling things I had ever seen. He told me that I called him the day before he had planned to go through with it. He said, "Everything was all planned out and set up. I didn't want to come here. I was planning to be gone, then you called." He went on to tell me that he heard genuine compassion in my voice on the phone that night. He said he trusted me. He remembered me saying that I thought he should come and also that I loved him. With tears dripping off his face, he said, "This trip is saving my life."

That night in the hotel was something I will never forget. Intense inner healing was taking place right in front of me. Chains shattered that day, and the rest of the trip was a celebration from that point. Neither of us expected that the next few days would be even better. I witnessed within myself, and by watching others, how powerful these insights can be in the hands of hungry and capable people.

The conference emphasized the empowering importance of understanding the Six Human Needs, as Mr. Robbins defines them. Although not commonly known in academia for his work on this subject, I feel like his contribution is masterful. Here's some of what we learned at the event.

The 6 Human Needs

Regardless of culture, demographics, or life experience, all of us have the same basic human needs. These things are not merely desires; they are needs. In some way or another, people will find a way to meet their needs. Every behavior that we engage in is in some way an effort to meet one, if not several, of these needs. We stop carrying out actions when they no longer meet any of our needs, but we cling to behaviors that do. When a need is not well satisfied, we will act out in some way, desperate to rectify the deficit. There are many positive ways, neutral ways, and negative ways to meet each need. Often time, we source harmful methods because they usually deliver faster results.

Think of these six needs as buckets. When our life is healthy, totally stable, and fulfilled, all six buckets are full of water. The problem is that each bucket has a crack in it, which causes the water to leak out over time. Some of it gushes out rapidly, some seeps out slowly, but none of the levels are static. We must continuously work to replenish each one to maintain optimal levels. As they become empty, we become more frantic to get them refilled. Let's label our buckets now.

Need #1 – Certainty

Certainty is one of the most fundamental and basic human needs. It's what some would call a survival need. We must have some security in knowing what to expect around us. The need for certainty pertains to food, shelter, and personal safety, but also to emotional stability. We must be confident that we can avoid danger and pain. Unconsciously, we work tediously to fortify this need. Whenever our certainty is in jeopardy, we will react to protect it.

We can meet the need for certainty in many ways. Working out and eating healthy every day could give someone certainty that she will live longer or avoid feelings of guilt and shame for being overweight. Working long hours at work may provide someone with certainty by having more financial security. Maintaining a dating relationship with another person, even if it's a lousy one, can make me certain that I will not be lonely. On the flip side, never dating anyone could give me certainty in knowing that no one will cheat on me ever again.

People perceive and value certainty differently, so we seek to fulfill it in different ways, driven by different priorities. Anger and aggression can be ways to achieve certainty. If a person despises the unknown and enters an uncomfortable situation with others, acting out in anger often provides some sense of control. Knowing how you will act is often a way to control how others will react. Fleeing the situation every time is a different way to control the outcome and be certain how it ends. Blame or victimhood could be ways to avoid uncomfortable feelings of guilt. These types of repeated behaviors become patterns as we try to fill our needs. Over time, the story we craft and continually tell ourselves also starts to become part of our identity.

When a situation gets shaky, some people turn to God for their certainty, while someone else may turn to drugs and alcohol. Drinking too much meets the need quickly because it's predictable. We know what to expect. Becoming drunk provides a particular place to hide and be numb for a while. Even depression and anxiety can be ways to get certainty. In the instance of depression, we know what to expect because we have done it before. We know that we can focus on ourselves and crawl into a familiar place to escape. Even though it's a miserable place to be, it is more comfortable for many people than the potentially dangerous place they might end up, like heartbreak or rejection. Cigarettes or junk food can provide certainty by allowing a moment of comfort or relaxation. Some may achieve certainty by never leaving the house, remaining protected from potential emotional or physical danger.

Being a good spouse can provide certainty, knowing that your partner has no reason to leave if her needs are being met. Some people can be sure that no matter what happens, they will figure it out. Many people are confident in their discipline or endurance. Someone else may know with certainty that no matter what happens, Daddy will come to the rescue.

Need #2 – Variety (Uncertainty)

Even though the need for variety may initially seem contradictory to the need for certainty, it makes sense with a little more thought. If everything were predictable all the time, we knew what was coming, and could manipulate things to remain constant, what would happen? In time, we would get very bored. This tendency creates the need for variety. We innately want to see and do new things. We naturally despise complacency. We desire discovery, learning, and stimulation. Staying in one place forever provides some certainty but leaves the variety bucket empty, which is not sustainable indefinitely.

Just like all the needs, there are wise ways and foolish ways to meet the demand for variety. You can get variation by reading a book on a new topic, or by starting a new business. It can be satisfied by hanging out with new friends, or by buying groceries you've never tried before. A promotion at work can temporarily fill the bucket, as can moving into a new house or buying new clothes. Seasons on the calendar provide variety, as do seasons of life. One of my favorite ways to add to my variety bucket is to travel.

Some people get bored and reach for drugs, alcohol, or other means to change their state quickly. Cheating on a spouse is despicable, socially unacceptable, and illegal, but it happens all too often because of needs not being met. A new fling every week certainly provides some variety. A deficit in variety can be very dangerous, just like the other needs. We must find safe and beneficial ways to meet the need to protect against harmful, desperate reactions. Stirring the pot is great, but only if we use the right ingredients.

Needs are satisfied differently for different people. It's a mistake to assume that two people prefer the same outlets for meeting needs. Social gatherings and meeting new people could threaten the need for certainty in some people, paralyzing them with anxiety. But the same situations could happily fill the variety bucket and produce joy for someone else.

Need #3 – Significance

The third human need is significance. This is the need to feel important, influential, unique, or valued. We have a desire to be recognized for our best qualities and achievements. We want to be respected, noticed, heard, and understood, even if we claim to dislike attention. Everybody needs to feel special.

We see people seeking significance by having the most expensive car, the fanciest clothes, the biggest biceps, the most tattoos, or the coolest friends. Others may be sure to let the world know that they are the smartest, gayest, most talented, or quirkiest member of the group. Standing out in a crowd can make us feel special. Competition and achievement undoubtedly fill the need for significance for many people.

Unfortunately, anger can also be a source to fill the bucket. If no one is paying attention to me, I can yell, cuss, and throw things. Then suddenly, people are focused on me, and I matter a little bit more. I can feel important by abusing other people, physically or verbally. It makes me feel powerful in a perverse and despicable way. Waving a gun in a crowded arena forces people to pay attention to me. Suddenly, I am the most significant person in the room. The need for significance is one of the leading forces driving violence, war, and terrorism. The reason the overwhelming majority of terrorist activities and

131

bar fights involve men is that aggression and dominance are primarily driven by testosterone, which is much more elevated in masculine people. Many men will die for significance and have proven so for centuries.

The bizarre thing is that if we cannot get the world to see us, pay attention to us, or affirm us, we will still find a way to meet the need alone. We have the capacity to make ourselves feel important with our own internal dialog. Self-pity, depression, and anxiety can all fill the need for significance too. In trying to meet needs alone, we often make ourselves feel important through suffering. Some people brag about their anxiety or depression as if they are competitive sports, as though having more severe neurosis is a trophy. Having more panic attacks and more crippling fear than someone else can make me feel special. The thing I hated most about my depression was when I finally recognized how selfish I was. Continually thinking about one person (myself) for extended periods was a shameful realization. I hated it, but it met a need. When the person who matters most is me, there will always be trouble. When multiple people do this within a group, it's a disaster.

Most people find a way to feel significant by having significant problems. Problems are more readily accessible than legitimate success. We get addicted to problems because they meet this particular need, and some of the others, so well. The issues eventually integrate into our story. After telling the story enough times, we permanently attach the problem to our identity. I'm not immature; I'm chemically imbalanced. I'm not fat; I'm big-boned. I'm not an underperformer; I've just never been given a chance. I'm not lazy; I am oppressed.

I've had plenty of deceptions in my own story. I thought I was so unique that I could never be understood. I believed that I could never measure up to the ridiculous expectations of the people around me. I told myself that I had so few sincere friends because people were all too superficial. I accepted that my ADD prevented me from attaining specific goals. These were all lies, but I repeated them enough to make them seem nonfictional in my story. We love our problems because they protect us from scrutiny. They create a longstanding, more dangerous problem. The story that shelters us can become the same one that eventually imprisons us. Be smart about which story you choose.

I don't mean to paint significance in such a poor light. The need for relevance is not bad. It's just potentially dangerous when we are in deficit and cannot find beneficial ways to meet the demand. Many of the ways we go about filling the bucket are reckless, selfish, and ego-driven. The quickest and easiest path is usually destructive and unsustainable. There are also positive ways to meet the need, just like all the other needs. Significance can be a powerful force for good.

We could get significance from being the most charitable person in our organization or the most generous person in the neighborhood. We can feel special by the way we care for children or the elderly. Your devotion to something beautiful, like a spouse, family, or friends can fill the bucket continuously. Self-sacrifice can make us feel like a hero. Discipline, patience, fiscal responsibility, or morality can all be sourced to fill the need too. We can adopt or care for innocent animals to feel significant, which is typically much more comfortable than caring for humans.

Being a recycling environmentalist can fill the bucket, but so can condemning those who are not one. Attending rallies and marches for ideological causes can make someone feel significant, but protesting them could do the same. The same paradox applies to many virtues that create identity. We must be conscious of how we get attached to the feelings of significance, so we do not travel down a destructive path. Hatred of the rich is not the same thing as love for the poor. Both have the potential to meet the need for significance in different ways.

Need #4 – Love and Connection

Regardless of what we may lie to ourselves and say to avoid pain, there is a deep desire in all of us for human connection. We need to love and to be loved. We need to get involved in other people's lives and also allow others to be involved in ours. We likely want to control just how involved, and on what terms, but we have a never-ending need to be together with other people. We remain deeply connected to others by human experience, whether through joy or suffering.

Most of us settle for connection because love is difficult, scary, and risky. Love pays higher dividends than connection but requires more vulnerability and courage. Many opt for connection because love was too painful in the past. We can satisfy this need through things like quality time, recreation, social gatherings, clubs, sports teams, conversation, cooperation, etc.

Just like the other needs, if we don't adopt sustainable, positive means to fill this bucket, we will find negative ways to do it. Commiserating with people over anger and disgust is undoubtedly a way to connect. Negative gossip with friends can do it too. As twisted as it may sound, physical fighting and abuse can even be a way to connect. Some people tolerate violence because they feel that it is still better than no connection, no significance, and being ignored.

There is no substitute for human bonding and intimacy. It's a requirement to be personally connected, on some level, for all humans. Love is not a state of mind or a feeling; it's a decision. You don't fall into it; you ascend into it. Real intimacy and deep human connection come through self-giving. Love is not self-seeking. It's the realization that someone is more important than yourself. We'll talk more about love and relationships later. For now, know that love and connection can be the driving forces in life because of basic human needs.

Need # 5 - Growth

The need for constant growth is useful and probably a little less dangerous than the previous four needs. We continuously need to improve, expand, and get stronger. If we are not growing, we know deep down that we are wasting. Not living up to our full potential hurts us. Wasting life produces guilt, resentment, anger, and shame. Conversely, our lives are better when we are making measurable progress. Progress is a phenomenal fuel for life that makes more satisfaction and fulfillment possible. I believe that influences our happiness more than any other variable. As long as we are achieving and moving toward new goals, we can feel fulfilled. The person you become can make you happy; the material things you acquire most likely cannot.

Our intelligence, character, and competence should continuously develop and improve over time. Growth contributes to the formation of our identity and validates that we are living well. It ushers us toward the best version of ourselves, and we can have peace knowing that we are adding valuable components to life and discarding useless ones.

Need #6 - Contribution

The final of the six needs is one that runs deep. The need to contribute to the betterment of other people is more of a spiritual or metaphysical need. We need to share good things with others. We need to help them make their lives better, uplift them using our experiences, and help them by using what we've learned—all of which gives more meaning and value to our lives. Life is better when we can give our best and see other people gain from it.

Offering our time, talents, and treasures to someone else is beneficial to both parties. We need to grow and give to have any chance of experiencing true fulfillment. Being conscious of the people around us and contributing to their success and happiness strengthens our connections and betters our worldview.

Fulfillment is possible when we start giving to something bigger than ourselves. It's possible to donate wealth or expertise to meet the need for significance. But when we can connect with others in a spirit of humility, knowing that someone else is more important than us, contribution flourishes. The same gestures take on different meanings when in a different mindset. The desire can shift from wanting credit for every deed to sincerely enjoying being a giver. There is no need for outside approval once we settle into the right frame of mind. We elevate into a higher state of being where service trumps status.

Know Your Needs & Know Yourself

Pondering these six needs will require extended thought and attention, but right now, think about which of these six needs you value the most. I don't mean which ones you practice well or which ones you know are starving for. Which ones do you value the most? Take a few minutes to pause and ponder it. There is no right or wrong answer. Everyone has a different response based on who and where they are. Identify your top two now before reading on.

1. Certainty
2. Variety
3. Significance
4. Love and Connection
5. Growth
6. Contribution

The two items in the list that you value the most probably influence and control the majority of your daily thoughts and behaviors, even more so than anything else in the external world. We craft stories and interpretations of everything in life, based on our hierarchy of needs and the current supply of each of them. My current top two needs are variety and growth. I am constantly learning better ways to meet these needs and ways to combat impulsiveness in an effort to do so.

There is no question of whether or not we will continually seek to meet these human needs. The real question is: How will we attempt to satisfy them? We should take some time to reflect on what we have done in the past to meet our needs, particularly the habits that we would like to replace. It's easy to remove behaviors that aren't meeting needs, but difficult to abandon the ones that are satisfying them. If the habit is hard to stop, it's likely because it meets multiple needs. Think about a recurring thought or behavior of your own that you despise. What needs could it be meeting? What would it take to get rid of it?

We are no longer depressed when all of our needs are satisfied. We don't bail out of a relationship when all of our needs get met either. Have you ever experienced a period of life when all of your buckets were full? Which ones have never been filled?

One action can often meet multiple needs simultaneously. Robbins teaches that when any behavior meets three or more needs at the same time, it can become an addiction. Getting together to gossip and trash talk other people can meet the need for variety, significance, and connection. Yelling at coworkers, employees, kids, or your significant other could meet multiple needs at the same time too. It could meet the demand for certainty by allowing control of the room, for significance by making you feel powerful, and for connection because at the moment, you are undeniably connected. Pornography could meet the need for connection, certainty, and variety in a perverse way. Doing drugs with friends could achieve the same three. Fortunately, we can get addicted to beneficial activities just as quickly as dangerous ones. We must create and control our habits, so they do not control us.

There are so many other psychological models for understanding human behavior, and it's likely beneficial to explore them too. Knowledge is power. Seek it out. But if we are to use this specific model for understanding ourselves, we must take some time to evaluate our six buckets.

Which one runs chronically low?

Which one seems to evaporate the fastest?

Which one threatens us the most when it's low?

Which produces the most stability when it's full?

After some exposition and contemplation, we can go a step further to ask which behaviors need a supplement or a replacement.

What are the negative ways we are meeting needs?

What are the better methods we could adopt to accomplish the goal?

Control over our reactions and emotions produces a higher form of certainty than hiding. Nine times out of ten, the better choice will be harder and take longer, which is precisely why we get stuck in troublesome spots.

If we desire to master self, to achieve growth, and to contribute more, we must press on. Take courage to face yourself. Strip down the persona, which is the fake, manufactured self, and discover your true self. Rewrite the story. Persona comes from the Greek word for mask. Take off the mask and take in the panoramic view now possible. Seeing the truth is not about self-hatred or shame. All your experiences are part of your formation. They are valuable for what is happening today and what will happen tomorrow. They were necessary to get you to the place where you are now. Now let's put them to use. Don't let them waste. Reconcile with your old mistakes, then move away from them. Depression can result from knowing that you have never ventured out of your comfort zone. It's time to explore outside of it and realize that the climate is better in new locations. A state of lesser anxiety comes after confronting the true self because we are no longer afraid of being exposed. Friedrich Nietzsche famously declared, "The strength of a person's spirit would then be measured by how much 'truth' he could tolerate, or more precisely, to what extent he needs to have it diluted, disguised, sweetened, muted, falsified." The truth will set you free, but only after it makes you uncomfortable.

To better understand self and be able to make positive, permanent change, we must take 100% ownership of our emotions. If we fail to take ownership, we set ourselves in a position to remain a victim. In blaming, we give away our power and our capacity to control the outcome. One of the only things we can control in life is our effort. We must keep pushing. The more we understand why we do what we do and continuously take inventory on where we are on the needs spectrum, the more we can grow. Through the process of education and reflection, we can better understand our tendencies and evolve into a better version of ourselves.

When I find myself in an unexpected emotional slump, I find it valuable to sit alone and ask a few questions. After an outburst, a bad day, or just realizing that I am in a low-energy funk, I now force myself to change my state and then sit with a list. I break the pattern with physiology first, followed by a deliberate change of focus. Before discussing it with someone else, I need to talk it over with myself. Here are some useful, sometimes uncomfortable questions I keep in my queue.

- What triggered these emotions?

- What need am I craving? (Which is code for, "Which one is in deficit?")
- What harmful thought is recurring or staying around?
- Why do I feel threatened?
- Who do I need to pardon or forgive?
- Does this behavior or state match up with my standards?
- What do you hate right now?
- What do you fear?
- What does your family or community need you to do?
- Where is the opportunity in this scenario?
- What happens if I stay here? Who does it affect?
- What happens if I transcend the problem?
- Who benefits from a corrective action?
- What are some positive ways I can fill the low bucket?

I need a big enough reason to escape selfishness and to stop wallowing in self-pity. Otherwise, I overstay my visit to the self-destructive destination that ends up hurting people. It's so easy to descend into a dangerous place when needs aren't satisfied. Stress is often the word over-achievers use for fear. Stress happens when my plan is not manifesting in the real world. So, what needs to change? The plan, my actions, or my interpretation of how things are unfolding? Stress will come, but there are remedies for it. We must get better at the honest diagnosis and management of anxiety, so it is alleviated quickly. It must be intercepted and dismantled. If it stays too long, it turns into suffering. Suffering is when we are stressed and anxious and feel powerless to change it.

These intimate, self-journeys require more time in solitude and away from distraction to process appropriately. Much of the task concerned with self-examination is averted by staying in a group and avoiding being alone. But if we can understand the six human needs and keep tabs on our own buckets, we are able to respond quickly. This helps us prevent unnecessary chaos and to maintain more peace and order. Regular checks help to intercept incoming problems.

Self-work is alienating and humiliating, as it should be. The wiser and more holy people in human history seem to be extremely humble. We cannot grow without admitting that we are wrong and needy. The more attached we are to the crafted persona, the harder it will be to sever from it. We must not be hypocrites, demanding one way from others, but excusing ourselves from the rules and standards we tout. The word hypocrite is rooted in the Greek word that means stage actor, pretender, or dissembler. We must stand on our own and ground ourselves in higher standards than those we expect of others. In this, we find the authenticity and vulnerability essential for growth. This work is never finished, and fortunately so because it can help to fill all of our buckets.

We must acknowledge our natural capacity for evil, and respect it, but also see the enormous potential for goodness. Keep the ego in check and monitor emotional progress. Accept feedback from the people who love you and want the best for you, but not from everyone. Ask what you want from yourself, the true self. Ask what you want for others. Just do you and do it well. You are no longer competing with anyone else. You should now compare yourself today against the person that you were yesterday and the one you plan to be tomorrow.

Cheers to you on your conquest. That is water in your chalice, right?

CHAPTER 9
Lost Leaders - R & R & L

Pills won't cure your stress and anxiety. They may temporarily mute or delay unwanted symptoms, but the ailments remain. Changing behaviors is the prescription with the power to heal stress and anxiety. We will now discuss three immediately gratifying, non-pharmaceutical solutions to these problems. It's now time for rest, recreation, and leisure to become three of your best friends.

A successful life requires work. People of your caliber don't need any convincing of that. What you may need, however, is to unpack, understand, and be reminded of the dire need for proper rest, recreation, and leisure. These are three different things with separate goals, focus, and outcomes. They'll likely require some mental retraining to get right.

This chapter is not a message to reiterate that we all probably work too hard, too often, with too many distractions. That sermon, albeit warranted, is already overstated. Those overworking tendencies are widespread cultural issues, no doubt. But they can certainly be dismantled by an individual with a sound mind and a capacity to think for herself. All of us are quick to generalize the widespread problems of overworking and distractions. However, we may not be able to deconstruct the "why" of it all quite so easily. Why do people over-work? Why do you? It may be for selfish reasons like prestige, notoriety, or power, striving to fill the significance bucket. Some less noxious desires would be things like safety and security, which may fit into the certainty bucket.

Whether or not they're conscious of it, many people work long hours to remain distant from other pain. Some of us use the office to hide, to avoid harder, more emotionally intense work, like being a good spouse, parent, or friend. It's easier to stay busy and distracted. After all, when we are visibly exhausted, we are more protected from expectations and scrutiny. We often use our distress and helplessness to disarm our critics.

There are many reasons for over-working. Some are good, and some are terrible. We need some rhythm and balance in our lives instead of peaks, valleys, crashes, and emergency recoveries. How you feel determines how you think. How you think determines how you feel. And navigating the two requires a strategy; we've got to have a plan to combat both sides. Rest, leisure, and recreation, all provide needed balance to an otherwise hectic and unpredictable life. Each is valuable in its own way and deserves our respect and attention.

First, I want to make sure we're on the same page. Since there are many definitions and even more interpretations of leisure, rest, and recreation, let's take a closer look at each one and define how it fits within this conversation. We'll grapple with leisure first.

Leisure

Please don't be confused about leisure. I don't merely mean rest, quiet, or a simple cessation of work—I'm talking about *purposeful* leisure. It's a disciplined action, not laziness or mindless filler. Aristotle made the point that our culture does not suffer from an overabundance of leisure, as many people are quick to diagnose. Instead, it suffers from "never knowing her at all." The thing that we often confuse with proper leisure is what he calls "amusements." Those are the short breaks and welcomed distractions that happen alongside work. These moments are necessary, but they do not require much of us. Aristotle says, "Amusements are more to be used when one is at work, for one who exerts himself needs relaxation, and relaxation is the end of amusement, and work is accompanied by toil and strain… we should be careful to use amusement at the right time, dispensing it as a remedy to the ills of work."

Examples of such amusements would be a snack break, a few minutes playing a puzzle game on the phone, a funny text exchange, or a conversation at the water cooler. The point of amusements is just a quick mental break, a breather, and a maneuver to distance ourselves from intense work for a few minutes to prevent mental and emotional gridlock. These moments are typically enjoyable for the simple fact that they allowed us to stop working. Our minds need them, especially when doing intensely focused tasks for long periods. I try to insert an amusement break of some sort at least every 45 minutes, even if it only lasts a minute or two.

In contrast, to be at leisure is choosing to be free for an extended period, without the immediate need to return to the work task. It's not a part of normal working at all. In proper leisure, no one else is demanding your time, thought, or energy. And when it's a deliberate choice—planned and not resulting merely from happenstance—leisure is beneficial to both body and mind. Good leisure is intentional, unrushed, and unencumbered time. It is enjoyable for the simple fact that it is in no way burdensome.

Leisure frees you to pursue activities aimed at cultivating your virtue and character. Real leisure not only affects what you are doing, but who you are becoming. Properly executed, it produces growth of the mind and spirit by allowing free-thinking in open time and space. The goal is to be unbothered. Leisure creates an uncrowded, unrushed pocket of space for something beautiful to enter, or it can simply be enjoyed as a void. It is a peaceful place to *be*. Leisure, as far as this book is concerned, should be willful. The intent matters. The "why" comes first, followed by the "how." The "what" is probably the least important. Socrates referred to real leisure as "the most valuable of possessions." When you get it right, you see improvements in every aspect of life.

I sucked at proper leisure before my transformation started. I despised it and thought it was a waste of time. On my list of priorities, it was probably on the bottom row. I misunderstood what it is and what it's for. I falsely assumed that it detracted from productivity, never appreciating that it improved my thinking, character, and success. I never desired extended pauses because I thought my best use of time was to keep cranking out good work. But through practice, I trained myself to love being still and to enjoy unscripted inaction. I now know that when executed well, leisure makes me a better person, more alive, and more aware. It also keeps me sane, motivated, and capable of operating at a higher level. Now, leisure is firmly placed higher on my priority list because I know I cannot do peak work without it. The non-taxing moments of freedom are nourishing.

If your focus is 99% work and 1% leisure, you won't make it very far. You will eventually stall or burn out. If productivity always trumps personal wellness, you will implode. We must make an intentional shift and give leisure a place of prominence in our heads, in our hearts, and on our calendar. Our culture is starving for this but fails to see it. We crave deep and meaningful conversations that produce change. We need to have these exchanges with ourselves and with others. We also long to discover the virtue that, deep down, we believe exists in ourselves and others. Leisure may help us to see more clearly what we need to do because the focus is on something more significant and pure. It transforms our work because we can connect with "why" we want to do it differently. Our work can then become a more purposeful form of duty and sacrifice. Unfortunately, we are too busy for it. Our standards are too low.

Maybe some people cannot tolerate the thought of a half-day of leisure because of guilt, knowing that they haven't delivered sufficient work yet. In contrast, when you know you gave it your best and already put in the hours, you believe that you deserve some open space once in a while. The labor can be a satisfying way to ensure enjoyment in the leisure. The work must be done well first. Then leisure can be enjoyed. Fulton Sheen put it this way, "No amount of piety in leisure hours can compensate for slipshod labor on the job. But any honest task, well done, can be turned into a prayer." If you are religious, you can make leisure a form of prayer after good work. If you are not religious, you can make it therapy. Much like stretching after a long workout, leisure allows our minds to relieve tension and become more flexible. In time, we can appreciate that leisure is a superior use of time and energy because of the benefits it creates. We offer our best, in work and in leisure, continually improving so we can offer something even better in the next round. How we do things and the mindset that goes with them matter, and the same job can mean more with a change in attitude and consciousness.

The goal of leisure is to be able to offer a better version of yourself by simply learning how to be. Leisure should have no measuring stick or grading system. It should be what it is: dedicated time to be. Amazing things can happen when we allow such space.

Leisurely Practice

- What if you decided to stop, look, and listen to your life and the lives around you?
- When was the last time you kicked back on a towel in the sun or rocked on the porch without a phone or an agenda?
- What if you made a reservation to visit with a friend without any time constraints?
- What if you used your weekend to connect with yourself or the people that you love?
- Doesn't your mind need something else to do besides work?
- What if you stopped talking for a while and started listening?
- How would it feel to enjoy some fresh air on top of a kayak for a few hours?
- Can you take a half-day this weekend to be alone in the park?
- What if you learned how to make leisure work for you instead of working to find leisure?
- How about taking a sick/vacation day off to sit and read a book or get a massage?

You don't have to have the flu to take a day off. Take one for a superior reason, one that could prevent the flu.

Hunting and fishing, both alone and with others, have always been a big part of my life. For many years, I thought it resonated on such a deep level because of the primal connection. Gathering clues, putting in the work, stalking the game, and bringing it home so the tribe can feast is very fulfilling. Delivering a cooler full of healthy meat to the soup kitchen fills my significance and contribution buckets for sure. It's all an adventure. But I now realize that there is a broader reason for my affinity for those activities. Nestled in between the adrenaline rushes is a substantial amount of quiet, sitting among beautiful scenery. I'm hard to reach; there's no cell phone coverage in many of the places I roam. These remote locations in the wild are places of pure leisure for me. They are medicinal. Quiet time with extended territory allows an opportunity to see how small I am and how incredibly complex the world is. It gives me time to think and to listen. When I return from an excursion, I am a better clinician, father, brother, son, friend, and husband. Very few things outside of leisure can be described that way. Leisure done well makes life better. Open spaces, whether physical or mental, provide opportunities that we need to think, relax, and be.

Purpose alone has the potential to change everything. When you set out for a period of leisure, know why you are entering this space. It should be a departure from normal life, so disconnect and stay awhile. Don't be discouraged if you fail to see immediate results or if it feels unnatural. Like every habit, purposeful leisure takes time and practice.

Rest

You know what rest is and know everyone needs it. But I'm not merely talking about sleeping; I'm talking about recovery. Your body has a fascinating ability to self-repair if you give it what it needs to do so. You need to rest in order to recover from grueling work. Sure, this happens when you sleep, but that's not enough. You also need time to recuperate outside of sleep.

A few days of rest time is critical for building muscle and strength in the gym. Without giving your muscles adequate time to recover, you can actually negate the gains from the workout or even regress. Life is no different. After a week of hard work or even a weekend of staying up late, your body needs rest to prevent a downward spiral. After intense work,

149

stress, eating unhealthy food on the go, or working your mind to the breaking point, you have to rest. If you don't, you can't recover and, in time, will suffer lasting damage. You need rest, even if you don't feel sleepy.

Listen to your body. You know when your mind, your back, or your spirit needs rest. Sometimes you need a withdrawal from a particular person or practice. One of my wife's preferred rest activities is to book a room at the hotel five miles from our home and take 24 hours to chill and recover. The goal is to be unavailable and unneeded. Her mind and body can truly rest there, knowing I have everything under control at home. She rests by reading, watching TV, and eating great food that she doesn't have to prepare.

The point of rest is simple: to recover. Pushing through the exhaustion and moving right onto the next project is a sure path to failure, burnout, stress, and anxiety. We must remain disciplined enough to shut everything down and recover after a season of hard work, abuse, trauma, or neglect. Be smart about it. Don't voluntarily take on difficult things when you are inadequately rested. Rest to be your best.

Recreation

Have you ever taken the time to even think about the word *recreation*? Re-creation! It means to create again, and If we do it right, recreation is regenerative. It is challenging to separate recreation from play, and there's no need to do so for the sake of this discussion. Let's make recreation and play synonymous for now.

Children know how to play. No one has to teach them to run, skip, or roleplay. They create games, use their imaginations, and naturally gravitate to playing, both alone and with others. They have an inclusive mindset and look for opportunities to gather others into their games. What happens to those natural desires and tendencies? Where do they go as we age?

Too many adults have forgotten how to play in our efforts to be all grown up. I would even go as far as to say that playfulness gets stolen from us. Not only do we forget how to do it well, but we become blind to its value. We replace purposeful recreation with meaningless distractions or more work. Instead of being together playing, which deepens friendships, intensifies relationships, and forges a sense of unity, we elect to keep busy alone. Many people get a chance to resurrect their love of play when they have children, but all too often, even that opportunity gets wasted.

Play is exhilarating. It makes you feel alive and connected. Why is there a need to remind you of this? Playing inspires thrills, enjoyment, and discovery. It can be physically demanding or relaxing. It spurs cooperation and community. Play grows your individuality and creativity. It expands your mind and vision. If you are serious about your work, play needs to be a substantial component in your routine. To become the best version of yourself, you must once again learn to play.

Like so many others, I crave recreation and competition. For so long, I experienced them mostly solo, through powerlifting, fishing, art, or entrepreneurship. Then, through adventure racing, group workouts, board games, and team sports, I rediscovered the joy of comradery and cooperation that accompany team activities. Those actions produced much fruit and fortified a deeper longing for more community involvement surrounding play.

My wife and I started inviting groups to our home for the lofty purpose of play. Sometimes it's entire families, and sometimes it's just the adults. For our annual couple's bocce tournament, we invite about a dozen teams. We lay out four courts in the back yard and play the double-elimination bracket all afternoon. At the end of the tournament, we have an award presentation, complete with fireworks. The winning team gets their name engraved on the obnoxious, gold cup trophy and keeps it until the next year when they return to defend their title. One year we had torrential downpour mid-tourney. We deliberated about a rain delay and ultimately decided to stay on the courts, which turned to sloppy mud pits in short time. We destroyed my manicured lawn but had a blast trudging through in the goop and splashing bocce balls. It looked like a scene from Woodstock.

But as much as we love play dates now, it took some time for them to take off. The first time we tried it, we rented a giant inflatable water slide and invited several families, telling everyone to bring their swim gear. Once the crowd started rolling in, my family realized that 100% of the children showed up ready to play, but only about 10% of the adults came to do so. While most of the adults sat on the porch drinking and watching from the cheap seats, my wife and I had big fun playing alongside the kids. Water slides are fun factories. If you are too adult for one, you're just too mature for me. The next time we held the same event, about 50% of the adults showed up with wet gear, ready to slide down the waterfall. By the third event, everyone came to play. Entire families were squealing in delight, tiring themselves out with belly laughs. The dads naturally made it into a competition, but all of us were winning, as individuals, as families, and as a community. It was recreation in the purest form. For a few minutes, no one was concerned with the difficulties of life.

It's now just expected that when you come to my house, we're going to play, whether it be a homemade slip and slide, pickleball on the driveway, kickball, or a water balloon fight. Some stay overnight to have a few meals together and play board games. A big breakfast together and a round of hide-and-seek or a few magic tricks are always a hit.

When we host game nights, we typically pick games that involve creative collaboration and problem-solving, something that I think people long for without realizing it. I also like to cherry-pick games that require some level of physical touch. I think we are dying for that too, both to give and to receive. (Relax, I don't mean a creepy or sexual type of touch.) Appropriate physical contact can be medicinal. It humanizes our experience and connects us on a deeper level.

People rarely realize that they naturally love the physical contact of sports for non-competitive reasons too. It's not just a battle of colliding muscles to see who is the stronger competitor. It's also good for the soul. The physical contact in basketball, rugby, football, soccer, wrestling, and so many other sports releases endorphins in our brains. I make it a regular point to grapple playfully with my children and my wife. We all benefit. Tickling sessions, back scratches, and cuddle times serve as forms of play, as well. I would not recommend tackling or tickling a stranger on the subway unless you are in need of blunt, heavy, physical touch to your face. But a reservation for a massage or a Jiu-Jitsu class may be in order.

Trying to get twenty people on the same schedule and value system is difficult. But luckily, one-on-one play is still great too. I invite a different friend over once a week to play and then rock on the back porch to chat. We tell funny stories while throwing a football or a Frisbee. Playing ping pong and talking philosophy is another favorite. Cooking a meal together or taking a short road trip can be recreational. It doesn't have to be extravagant or complicated.

Dancing is also a superior form of play for those brave enough. It's another activity tragically lost in adulthood that can be resurrected easily. It's fun with a partner or a crowd, but you don't need a wedding, a DJ, or six beers to move your body to music. The option is available almost anytime. Singing in the car or the shower is another form of play that requires no one else or any special gear.

If we aren't playing, it's because we have fallen asleep, been brainwashed, or become distracted from the fundamental

153

things that matter most. So, be an opportunist. Keep a disk, baseball gloves, a soccer ball, or a hackie sack in your trunk. Grab a friend and play catch during breaks at work or ask someone to join you afterward. Pick back up your abandoned hobbies of music, tennis, or painting. When's the last time you rode a bike, climbed a tree, or went roller skating? Why can't you play hide-and-seek anymore? Think like a kid, and don't overthink it. Just grab some people and play. Invite some folks to race go-carts or hit the trampoline park for some dodgeball. See what happens to your anxiety level when you joke around, play pranks, and stop taking yourself so seriously all the time. Purposefully recreate yourself, include others, and have some fun.

CHAPTER 10
The Path to Stillness - Meditation

MEDITATION HAS BECOME a trendy topic (again!). Maybe it has to do with the world's infatuation with self-enlightenment. Another explanation could be that meditation provides some people with a desired, quasi-religious experience that skirts concrete doctrine or morality. Or perhaps it's perpetually popular because our soul is just longing for some simple, peaceful, stillness in a world saturated with busyness and constant distraction. We all desire the positive benefits that we think accompany meditation. But unfortunately, meditation is often misunderstood, poorly represented, or mixed up in a slurry of many other buzzwords.

It's normal in today's world to never make time for meditation. It's common and acceptable to be distracted with a busy mind, wavering emotions, fidgety bodies, and impatient temperaments. No one will fault you for avoiding the discipline. They will never even notice you did since you will blend right in with the masses. What you will notice, as will the people that know you, is the contrarian person you become when meditation is inserted into a place of prominence in your life.

Meditation is difficult to define because it varies in between many religions and traditions, and often even differs among the practicing members. Most folks have blended some cocktail of Confucianism, Buddhism, Taoism, Christianity, Atheism, and whatever else you want to sprinkle in there. Unless you are a Tibetan monk or a Franciscan priest, you will likely have to develop an individual system and a specific practice that works for you. Having multiple hours every day without a career, a family, or bills to pay is probably not an option. I am not taking a stance that it is a luxury not to have these things. I do not wish to sit alone in one position or pray all day. I mention the contrast of "normal" life with monastic life because they are very different and therefore warrant different approaches. Grant yourself permission and patience to figure out your unique meditation process. As we highlighted before, your experience is incomparable to someone else's. Your meditation journey is your own and involves only one person.

Do me a favor. For a few minutes, try to ignore every prior emotion that you associate with the word meditation. If you have tried to get into it, you were probably left with some frustration, or at minimum, a sense of disenchantment. If you have never developed a lasting practice for meditation, you probably have some spiritual fantasy in mind that isn't practical. I don't want to quell your enthusiasm because meditation is impactful. The activity just needs to be approached with less grandiose expectations and an open mind, which you will see, is largely the point.

Zen Sin

Like most people who bail out early, my first several attempts at meditation were all a bust. I tried multiple methods for breathing, focus, and consciousness. I read many books and emulated people who were supposedly doing it well. But reading and doing are two different things, and instead of peaceful focus, my efforts only produced frustration and failure. The only thing I was concretely conscious of during my attempts was how much I hated wasting my time. Focusing on a single object didn't work. Using a pre-defined audible guide or a mobile app didn't work. Returning to the breath or concentrating on physical body parts didn't help me either. Counting was a joke.

One... too many distractions. Start over.

One, two, three... for God's sake, what am I doing? Try again.

One, two, three, four, five, six, seven... I ate the wrong lunch for this. Reboot.

One, two, three, four, five, six, seven, eight, nine, ten-der are my quads from this stupid lotus position. Never mind.

Meditation felt like a lost cause—until I found a straight-forward method that was infinitely simpler than all of those.

Clearing the Path

My breakthrough came when I realized there is a big difference between mindfulness, contemplation, and meditation. Unfortunately, these terms often get scrambled together, interchanged, or skipped over entirely. All three have different purposes and a different process for achieving those goals.

For the sake of brevity and clarity, let's define three loose terms now to eliminate confusing assumptions. These are my own definitions for the purpose of this book. I don't want to fight about them on Twitter.

Mindfulness = focusing attention and being present in the current moment. It involves being conscious and aware of something, maybe everything. It requires us to be "in the now" and to direct our focus toward a specific thing. That could involve a process of gratitude, taking a physical or emotional inventory, or simply knowing where you are sitting and why. Mindfulness attempts to appreciate what is currently happening, instead of dwelling on the past or planning for the future. That's certainly useful, as most things we are worried about have either already happened or will never happen. Mindfulness can also serve as a grounding tool to bring awareness to the present moment. That is particularly helpful when we are scatterbrained and over-busy, but only if we focus our awareness on the right things. And that's where mindfulness can get a little sticky: what we should be mindful of is not so easily defined.

Contemplation = thinking about thinking. Some groups even recognize it as a form of prayer. It is a process of training our minds to interpret and process differently. Contemplation requires education, time, courage, and honesty. It involves sitting with our beliefs and emotions, deciphering which ones need to be killed, which are beneficial, and which need modification or repair. It can be rewarding, uplifting, and encouraging at times. It can also be critical and ruthlessly painful. Both extremes are necessary for progress. Hopefully, contemplation is a call to action. It's one thing to understand how your parents' behaviors affected you; it's another thing to contemplate what you should do about it. We cannot arrive at a full understanding of problems or at brilliant solutions without this one.

Meditation = stillness. Why did you fidget and squirm in your seat just now? Does the word stillness cause you angst? It did for me. Meditation involves a totally passive approach, where mindfulness and contemplation are active. In meditation, we hope to make our minds still enough to create empty pockets of space, devoid of regular thoughts. Great things can happen in those gaps. During a typically hectic day, there is way too much competition for your headspace, creating a dire need for meditation. It creates the opportunity for more beneficial thoughts by shutting off all the noise. It reduces stress and anxiety and increases creativity and productivity. It has been proven to improve sleep and reduce depression. Some people recognize meditation as another form of consciousness.

Think of it as a form of super rest for the mind and a safe place to relax without being bombarded by an overabundance of thoughts. Meditation is a special reservation made for relaxation, recovery, and healing.

Plain and simple, meditation is necessary to become the best version of yourself. The problem is that it takes time to learn the skill, and we are impatient. Many of us have false expectations about the process and give up too early. To further complicate the issue, I think that once people arrive at a successful meditative practice, we forget how arduous the path was to get there. We talk about it like it's no big deal, and we expect others to know how to "just be." This leads others astray. The truth is that no one can step right into it on demand. It requires preparation. Like anything else of value in life, we must be willing to suck at it before we can be any good at it. And that's not easy for high performers.

Highly productive people need to remember that the point of meditation is to be better at life, not to get better at meditating. Meditation is not a competition or an identity. It is a part of daily life, just like eating, breathing, and sleeping. Remember, too, that being present is not the same thing as meditation. Some people will say that they meditate while cooking, playing golf, or painting. Those things are probably more akin to amusements or leisure, involving a mental break from one activity, but requiring a different form of brainpower for the other. Meditation is a break from all of that. Meditation requires stillness—and maybe that's why so many of us find it so uncomfortable.

More Brake and Less Gas

This is a good time to rehash that Blaise Pascal quote from earlier: "All of humanity's problems stem from a man's inability to sit quietly in a room alone." Why is meditation, which should be the easiest of everything you do all day, so difficult?

Is it in your DNA to be active?

Is it unnatural to be still?

Are you too aggressive and controlling to allow such passivity?

Are you afraid to be silent, worried about who or what you may encounter there?

Are you really too busy, or is that the easiest excuse?

Are you hiding from something?

Why is it such a struggle to sit?

It's important to ponder all of these questions, but seriously consider an implicit idea now. If life demands so much of you that you don't have the freedom to do what you know you need to do, like meditate, exercise, and play, you must admit that you are a prisoner. But you are not required to be powerless pawns trapped in someone else's game, or slaves to the whims of the world. We are free to choose another path at any time, opting out of standard chaos. Making time for meditation is as simple as choosing to do so. It's a decision that no one else can or will make for you.

I think we all have an innate desire for stillness; we are just terrible at pulling it off. It's almost like we feel guilty about taking the time. We need some acceptable excuse or a disguise for it. Here's an illustration to support my hypothesis. Have you ever thought about how strange it is that people love the beach in the summer? It's blazing hot. We repeatedly smear greasy lotion all over our bodies to avoid skin cancer while cooking our own flesh. We sit all day in the dirt, not on a beautifully manicured lawn. That dirt is the priciest real estate in the country, and it sticks to our sweat and greasy lotion. The wind blows sand in our faces. When we get too hot or too dirty, we can take a dip in water that burns our eyes and is full of aggressive and poisonous creatures. And we pay exorbitant amounts of money to do it! It sounds nuts when defined it this way. I love the beach just as much as the next guy, but I think we should ask why. Why do we love that place? Besides the extra vitamin D and the enjoyment of being mostly naked and people watching, there has to be more. I think we love the beach because we have an excuse to sit and do nothing without anyone judging us for it or feeling unproductive. I am not claiming that this is true meditation. I'm just pointing out that our bodies are capable of and do appreciate the act of being still. Where else could you do this? Should we take the time to sit more than once per year? Must we travel a few hundred miles to find our seat?

We can never enjoy stillness until we learn how to stop. It's hard enough to be physically still, but a mental pause is even more tricky. On the path to quiet, we have to learn how to eliminate a great deal of the ambient noise, which is easier said than done in our culture. Fortunately, I found a method that works for even the most stillness-adverse person out there. I know because it worked for me.

Methods for Madness

If the goal of meditation is peace and stillness, how do you arrive there? How can there possibly be a process that involves no process? Like targeting better sleep, nutrition, or physical fitness, meditation is one of those things that requires a decision. It requires faith in the process. Faith says, "It's worth the risk." Fear asks, "What if it's not?" Make a choice. The key, in the beginning, is deciding to show up. Here is the three-part formula I recommend:

1. Select a time of day and a set location where you will meditate every day.

2. Show up at the selected time, without a phone, a notebook, or a plan.
3. Just sit there!

If that sounds too simple, you are on the right track. I don't mean to be coy or irreverent, just clear. You don't need another to-do list, or to take a course on how to do this right. You don't need an app to guide you with a massage soundtrack. You don't need an uncomfortable position, to tune your chakra, or to tend to other esoteric subtleties. You need to show up and do the work, which is actually to do no work at all. Showing up *is* the work. How long should you do it? Francis de Sales said, "Half an hour's meditation each day is essential, except when you are busy, then a full hour is needed." I know, as do you, that you are not going to sit for an hour. Start with 20 minutes and faithfully do it without any excuses for two weeks. Just sit there! This simple act of discipline is an important starting place.

I committed to 20 minutes per day, and in the beginning, I hated every minute. I showed up sleepy and uninspired, which didn't help. I blended dosing off and struggling to meditate many mornings. Nodding off and accidentally spilling hot coffee in my lap did help break my tiredness, but a burning crotch rarely contributes to achieving any calm. The time sitting there was annoying, but I still showed up daily and put in the reps. Like many entrepreneurs and busy-bodies, I had so many thoughts in my head. There was no semblance of quiet or stillness. Even if I tried to be present, there were too many distractions in my mind. Luckily, I learned to buck the former advice I received on meditating. My prior foolish instructions taught me that thinking was terrible and that the point of meditation was to have zero thoughts. I was supposed to experience being, and that was all. If I could "just be" one with the universe, fate, and with God, then I was doing it right. *What does that even mean?*

If thoughts were wrong, I could never be right. I failed at that method, but not from a lack of trying.

I modified the process to work better for me. Instead of punishing myself for having thoughts, I accepted them. As thoughts entered my consciousness, I gave myself permission to entertain and cross-examine them. Instead of trying to cram them in an overstuffed trash can and pretend they weren't there, I would sit with them and then sort them. I had imaginary boxes for different categories. A memory, idea, or emotion would arrive, and I would ask a simple set of questions.

Is this useful?

Does this have a purpose in my life?

Is this benefitting me, teaching me something, or hurting my progress?

Then I would move the thought into the properly labeled bin. Some examples of my imaginary containers were:

Great Memories, Lies, Randomly Useless, Old Garbage, Possibly Brilliant Ideas, Needs More Exploring Later, and even one for Requires Immediate Attention. If something showed up needing expedited attention, I would put all the focus on that thing. Like a police interrogation, I would stare at the thing and ask questions of it, trying to find the source, a motive, and a plan to make things right. Some of my examples in this category would be contempt for a family member or employee, resentment, jealousy, fear, depression, disappointment, apathy, or hopelessness. Over time, more beautiful components started showing up, too, like joy, humor, love, belonging, and affirmation. Those were much more fun to examine.

I know what you are thinking, that this sounds like work and not stillness. You are correct, but before you label me a meditation heretic, understand that the intense work is temporary. It's necessary in the beginning. Your mind is a crowded storage shed crammed full of thoughts, ideas, emotions, trash, memories, and broken things. It's not really usable until you clean and organize the workspace. We can enjoy the 25 good things only after we remove the 700 that are causing the clutter.

Over several weeks, I got better at noticing and sorting. I stretched the twenty minutes to thirty. I showed up faithfully to my meditation chair every day, occasionally experiencing peace but usually feeling like I was doing work. After a few months, the thoughts started slowing down. (Yes, I said months.) That's when the better-quality stuff started showing up. The superficial, more frequent items dissipated, and the more significant concepts had space to roam freely. I'm still unsure whether the pace slowed down because so many thoughts had been sorted and put away, or whether I was training my brain to stop caring about so much senseless drivel. Either way, after a couple of months, I was finally experiencing real meditation. I lengthened the now-sacred time slot to forty minutes and was receiving tangible benefits from the dedicated time. I got to know myself better from all angles, the good, the bad, and the ugly. I started seeing other people differently, too. Most of them coincidentally got less ugly throughout the process.

Once the clouds began to roll away, I finally started to experience what I thought the monks and mystics were talking about. It wasn't often or predictable, but there were blissful pockets where I had no thought. These were the transcendental moments of tranquil stillness. To borrow Buzz Aldrin's iconic description of what it was like while standing on the moon, I think meditation is "magnificent desolation." I knew enough about life and suffering to understand that I shouldn't idolize these moments or make them the object of my desire. They were undeserved gifts that could not be predicted or expected. In the non-magical times, I was growing. Instead of trying to understand everyone else, I started to understand myself better.

Understanding human nature may be way more valuable than any statistics or lab results.

It's so hard to relax when we are in constant fight-or-flight mode, but sometimes we need to stop running and fighting in order to see anything clearly. Detachment, contentment, and security are all products of meditation in time. These elements make future sorting more efficient, so there is more time to chill. Free yourself from the daily barrage of emotions for a few minutes. They are exhausting. Give yourself permission to clock out for a while. Even if you can't fully relax yet, at least experience what it feels like to stop sprinting. Sit down, be still, and don't let anything slip by your consciousness that you need to experience. It's going to take a while to get to true calm, but know that the system is working, even if you don't feel tingly. Give it time. Show up and do the work.

A scheduled retreat may be a good idea to help jump-start the process. I place several of them on my calendar each year for maintenance. Physically removing yourself and going somewhere quiet, away from normal distractions and responsibilities, is usually a worthwhile endeavor. Just know that the work required will still be the same. There is no magic pill. Early in my psychological and spiritual journey, I decided to spend two nights at a monastery. This was a beautiful property where the only noises allowed were scheduled bells and monk chants. I am not a monk and was never given permission to pull the rope to ring any bells, so silence was my only option. After a full day struggling with the audible void, I walked down to the lake to sit alone. It was a blissful, almost spiritual moment in time, like most every time you sit alone by the water. A group of ducks gracefully swam across the lake. It was quiet. I was one with nature, with my consciousness gliding in unison with the gentle wake behind the animals. Well, at least until they reached the shore in front of me. It was then that I realized that these fowl had an agenda, and they were angry about it. I don't know if I was sitting beside a nest full of eggs, or if they knew I had smuggled bread rolls in my pockets, but they came in hot! Honking, flapping, and biting, they chased me across the green pasture. I broke the property by-laws as I screamed expletives and threw bread and sticks in an attempt to save my life. That night, I laughed as I mended my jeans and meditated on the harsh realities of natural chaos and order.

Preheating

Much like the mental cues for proper sleep, a consistent priming routine is beneficial before meditation time. This gives us neurotic performers something to do to satisfy our former addictions for activity and control. Whatever your setup, keep as many variables constant as possible so that your brain can learn the cues. For me, it's the same cup of coffee, the same chair, the same blanket, and the same reserved, quiet time each morning before everyone else wakes up. Find a neutral place where you cannot see 100 other things that need to be done. Get into a prime state by utilizing strategic physiology, focus, mindset, and language. Many people have a gratitude routine to get warmed up for meditation. I like to remind myself of the need for humility and emotional detachment beforehand. I still stink at both. Find a pre-game ritual that works for you.

Ignatius of Loyola taught a five-step practice called *The Daily Examen*, which I find is a solid primer for meditation. The Jesuit order Ignatius founded in the 1500s is known for its teaching to see God in everything, even the simple, mundane, or ugly things. There are many versions and iterations of *the Daily Examen*, but the basic model is straightforward.

Step 1 is to recognize the presence of God.

Step 2 is to give thanks and be grateful.

Step 3 is to review the prior day, assessing how we thought and acted.

Step 4 is to respond to our failures and shortcomings, recognizing what needs work.

Step 5 is to look forward to the day to come and approach it with more awareness and wisdom than yesterday.

A period of reflection like this takes some courage because it has the potential to reveal your weaknesses. But if you don't voluntarily expose them yourself, the world will do it for you, likely in an inopportune moment. Remember that the goal is stillness, not punishment. There will also be moments to highlight your strengths, which will steadily grow in number. Either way, be careful not to get too self-absorbed. In time, you will enjoy the detours through the emotional, intellectual, and even the spiritual. Hopefully, these pockets become opportunities to identify vices as well as opportunities. Seeing what you are doing is important. Understanding why you are doing them is even more beneficial. Use the six human needs model you learned earlier to assist in diagnosis. Privately ask hard questions and get to know your true self. Grant the tired stage actor a permanent vacation.

The goal of a healthy spirituality is to wake up. When it's working, we can more clearly identify what needs to be done. Once the work is done, we can be still and relax. But remember, the point of putting on your oxygen mask first is so that you have a sound mind to turn and help people around you. Show up and keep showing up.

Namaste.

CHAPTER 11
Lightening the Load - Minimalism

N OW THAT YOU'RE thinking differently and reconsidering emotional attachments, you can vault into a process for reducing stress and anxiety that provides immediate gratification. There aren't too many things in life that offer instant positive results, so don't pass up this one. It's time to minimize your excess burdens and significantly lighten your load.

Just like the physical body and posture we discussed earlier, our physical spaces directly affect our mind and body too. In a similar way that we discern our thoughts and emotions, removing those that are no longer useful, we must apply the same scrutiny for the physical objects in our lives. So many items get left in our local environment, haphazardly and unconsciously, simply because they have always been there. Others are left there because we have not had the time or focus required to deal with them appropriately. The accumulation of material possessions quietly compounds for years. It's a form of addiction that the culture doesn't prefer to discuss. Nonetheless, the coveting and hoarding is a stark reflection of our emotional and psychological conditions, both past and present. Minimizing those physical objects in our lives creates more peace, well-being, time, energy, and personal fulfillment.

There may still be a few elements that need to be added to supplement total emotional balance, but this chapter is all about subtraction.

Subtraction - Addition = Minimalism Math

We need to travel away from excess and clutter to appreciate the simplified freedom on the other side. That's the tricky part about minimalism: we don't yet have a full concept of what we want because we can't understand something that we have yet to experience. Living with freedom, margin, and space is an alien concept for most modern lifestyles. The initial step may be the hardest, but fortunately, momentum builds rapidly. Like any proper 12-step program, the initial step is admitting that there is a problem—and if you are living in a first-world country, especially the west, there is most likely a problem. Unless you have intentionally grappled with materialism, consumerism, and excess, the culture has been dragging you into the swamp since birth. I'm not saying that everything you own has to fit in one carry-on bag, which may be the ultimate goal for the turbo minimalist. More power to you if that's the target. But, even if you don't go to that extreme, there are plenty of areas that could use work. We all have too much stuff, and it's physically, emotionally, and spiritually holding us down. Now it's time to cut the chains and be set free. Improving our space improves our emotional state, and emotions influence our actions.

"If you have more things than you can manage, you have too many things." That was the line I repeated to my children over and over before minimizing our home. As I mentioned at the beginning of this book, I thought I was doing better than the people around me. That was the case for this category too. My household had less stuff than everyone else in our social circles. We made what I thought were conscious, rational spending choices. That gave me a sense of accomplishment. No one could have accused us of being hoarders, but that's not exactly a high bar, is it? After preaching, "You have too many things" to my children so many times, one day, I internalized it and began to reexamine my own spaces. Part of my stress, anxiety, depression, and failure were stemming from the fact that I had too many things to manage. I could not adequately handle them all. I certainly could not do it well, not with a healthy mindset. There was too much tension. I had too much stuff to live the life I wanted. Each item requires some level of time, energy, and attention to maintain.

I had too many projects, which required too many supplies and too much space. There were too many events on the calendar, which required too many beautiful things to get bumped. There were too many things to keep repaired and running. The to-do list was always too full. These things constantly interrupted my train of thought, telling me all the things I needed to do. They were stressing me out and disturbing my chi. I was seemingly doing better than my peers and the general population, but that was not good enough. I was too good to feel this bad. I wasn't renting storage units for my excess junk. I could still locate things in my garage when I needed them. I was even still one of those rare outliers who actually used the garage to park a car. But when I looked around, I still saw a lot of *stuff*. Culture is potently influential, and it had infected my family too.

If we are honest, much of our character gets wrapped around the things we own, crafting an identity that produces no return on investment. The other problem is that the things you own tend to own you. With every item we accumulate, there is more maintenance, less space, and less sanity. They create more burdens and distractions. But when we get rid of something, we create space and remove unnecessary items off the to-do list. We restore more sanity through simplifying.

A fruit tree requires cutting to yield the most fruit. Pruning the excess limbs and leaves allows all the resources to be channeled to the most desirable parts, allowing them to mature and be enjoyed. Ignore or forget to trim the tree, and you'll get less quality fruit. What I have learned about growing fruit, and also cultivating peace, is that many good things need to be removed to make room for better things. It's difficult for me to knock one-third of the early peaches off my trees. But that is the only way to grow fully mature ones that make it all the way to harvest. Selective pruning is an exact parallel to so many things in our physical and emotional spaces. Get rid of the bad, and even some of the good, to make room for the best. There are a finite number of resources available to us, and when they are spread too thin, everything suffers.

How many of the areas in your life could use a solid purging? How many forgotten, expired, or useless items are squatting in the attic, basement, garage, furniture, pantry, refrigerator, or plastic storage bins? How many pairs of brown shoes does a sensible person need? How many handbags, cookbooks, picture frames, golf clubs, books, jackets, files, collectibles, or heirlooms should we keep? Why do we feel a need to keep them? What would life be like if they disappeared?

Clutter is insidious and dangerous. It distracts us, frequently interrupting our necessary daily tasks. It produces guilt, highlights inadequacies, induces pain, and incessantly pesters us. It steals our energy and attention. Being surrounded by mess makes us increasingly more stressed and restless. How can we relax when there is so much to do? The more we have, the more we have to do. And even worse, the more we have, the more we seem to compare, compete, and to desire even more. Shopping and spending are drugs. Burying ourselves in stuff is a symptom of sickness.

Skeletons in the Closet? (and the Attic)

Outer order often reflects inner peace. Likewise, an external environment in disarray likely reflects internal chaos. We don't discuss it often, but we intuitively know that these concepts are true. An unhealthy amount of stuff reflects inner turmoil, whether the problem is spending, attachments, clutter, or a lack of organization. Thankfully, now that you are a mindful, contemplative person who meditates on such things, you can better diagnose why you needed so much stuff. Pondering the six human needs with a proper mindset will point to quite a few telling answers. Then, you can form a better plan to meet those needs and abolish the negative aspects of having too much baggage, both internal and external.

Everyone knows that things don't make people happy. New things don't stay new for long. The excitement of a luxury car wears off. Fashion trends move, just as they are designed to do. The thrills of certain activities wane as they become less novel. Even some of the relationships we chase go stale. Many of these material things meet short-term needs. But why do we keep stockpiling possessions that fail to produce any joy or even any admiration from others? What about the things we keep around that we no longer use, and no one ever sees?

It takes courage to be honest about our own negligence, shortcomings, and addictions. Gathering and hoarding objects reflect our anxieties and insecurities, pointing to areas that need work. Maybe we need to grieve, to let go, or to grow up. Perhaps we need to cultivate better systems or become more discriminating consumers. Maybe we need to examine the motivations behind our actions more thoroughly. Why do you have so much stuff? Why do you keep buying more? Are we attempting to manage old insecurities?

Perhaps the initial satisfaction of obtaining the items is less about holding the stuff, and more about acquiring it. Maybe having the option to buy something makes us feel powerful or special.

- Are you starving for significance, connection, or variety?
- Is this the way you give yourself gifts because no one notices how deserving you are?
- Is shopping and keeping piles of stuff around a form of distraction, or even self-sabotage, so you can stay busy instead of sitting still and dealing with harder things?
- Is having a messy abode the way you keep guests out?
- Is having a crammed schedule the same tactic?
- Which needs are being met?
- Which ones are in deficit?
- Where and why are you so needy?
- Why are you attached to the stuff?
- Why can't you get rid of it?
- What responsibilities are you avoiding?
- What emotions come with acquiring the stuff?
- What is the real addiction?

We must sit and ask ourselves many questions before we have the proper framing and motivation to clean up our act. Otherwise, the disposal is temporary, and the items return. We need to evaluate the physical things, as well as ourselves.

Maybe it would be wiser to drive a non-luxury vehicle that doesn't cause us to drive with road rage and park with paranoia. Perhaps we should rent the fancy gown for the big party and borrow the jewelry from Grandma instead of purchasing all of it to feel important. We too often buy things we don't need, with money we don't have, to impress people we don't like.

Many of us keep items around that we think we'll need later for our fantasy life. You know, when you get rich, when you lose weight, when you have more time, when you have more friends to come over, or when you have a grandchild?

Even if you lose the extra weight, you won't want those clothes later, anyway. They will be out of style, and you will want to reward yourself with something happy and new anyway. If you haven't touched the car or boat that you planned to restore for the last three years, haul it off. Life rarely gets less busy without serious intentionality. If you sincerely desire to entertain more at home and have friends over, the best way to make sure it happens is to have a space that's easier to keep clean. When someone sends a message that they are passing through town in 30 minutes and want to drop by, we should be delighted, not panicked. This is a prime example of something beautiful that quickly turns into a source of anxiety because of a poorly managed environment.

Some of us keep items around because they were expensive or hard to acquire. People will say, "I worked so hard to buy that." Well, congratulations. The good news is that you won't have to work so hard to eliminate it. Buying a thing that you won't use is mistake number one. Keeping it is mistake number two. It seems that the longer we own something, the harder it is to turn it loose. Act fast now to save grief later.

As with everything else in this book, the more you practice, the better you get at the craft. You learn how to properly place values on things and learn emotional detachment from them. Some items are no-brainers, and others take some time to process. Cleaning out your spaces clears your mind, whether a desk, closet, purse, to-do list, or storage building. A clean, uncluttered environment is more welcoming and more restful. We can then experience better leisure and meditation because there is no oppressive pile of stuff glaring at us from the corner.

Methods for the Madness

You can go about this in a variety of ways, and it does not all have to happen at once. Maybe it starts with a 10% elimination, and then after a few months, another 10% purge.

Some people empty an entire closet, cabinet, or dresser and place everything in the middle of the room. With the pile in full view, the items are then sorted, one by one, determining if they are useful, necessary, or life-giving. Does the thing produce delight or guilt? When is the last time it got used? Do you need it? Does it make you happy? What would life be like without it? This process could take a while. The key is having adequate time set aside to go for it.

Another method I hear people discuss is to remove one item every day. This method is more comfortable because it doesn't require as much time in one sitting, but it allows some people to only contend with the easy stuff. It also doesn't get you very far. It would take a lifetime to finish minimizing most homes with this tactic. Most of us need a more aggressive approach.

For my household, it happened rather abruptly and unexpectedly. We had kicked around the idea of paring things down and dabbled with the process a little bit, but nothing dramatic. That's when the major paradigm shift commenced. We were scheduled to go on a week-long beach trip when my very pregnant wife started having some complications. She was advised not to travel more than an hour away from the hospital. She still urged me to take all the kids and enjoy the beach, which made me nervous on multiple levels. While we were catching stingrays and building sand fortresses, she was turbo-nesting. I am not the only opportunist in the house, and she had a rare chance to do some major purging. She went hard-core on the home cleanout, releasing an unrelenting wave of tidy fury. I received many text messages with flexing-arm and fist-bump emojis throughout the week. She loved it. I cheered her on from afar. One day, she sent me a picture of my fully loaded truck headed to the donation center. Another pic followed on a second trip, and then again on the third. And those three loads were after she had already invited her friends to take what they wanted.

She didn't touch any of my personal items but went after everything else with gusto. By the end of the week, she had done every closet, cabinet, and storage bin. She told me to call her on my way home so she could explain everything to us via speakerphone. She informed us that things would look different when we returned home, but that we would love the changes. She asked us to try it out for a few weeks and told us that if we were missing something important to let her know.

We arrived home to a noticeably clean, simple, refreshing space. It was awesome. There were no emotional nuclear meltdowns. The kids liked their new spaces that were now easier to clean and maintain. They enjoyed their favorite things more with the extra space. It was an easy sell. Of the dozens of things that were placed on reserve, only one was ever missed or mentioned. One item! And it was fetched from the attic, where my wife had placed questionable items that she was hesitant about removing. The rest found their way to the donation center in time too.

After tasting the fruits of her pre-labor labor, I was inspired to get moving on my part. I blocked off adequate time and tackled my items, one space at a time, asking the questions I had learned from the resident pro.

- Do I need this?
- Is it life-giving?
- Does this help fulfill my life's purpose?
- What would life be like without it?

I did pretty well on my first pass and eventually came back for another round a few months later. The purging method I used is simple. When I decided to clean out my closets, I determined how many shirts, shoes, belts, and pairs of pants I legitimately needed. I decided that I needed two pairs of jeans. So, I selected my two favorites and got rid of all the rest. I needed one brown belt and one black one, so all the others were donated. I had way more polo shirts, pants, and button-ups than I needed. Half of them didn't fit well, or I didn't feel good wearing them. Those easily fit into the purge box to donate. Ladies, if you don't love the dress, you will not wear it. Just let it go. Now, when it's time to go out on the town or leave for a getaway, there is no indecisiveness in our home. We don't waste life away, standing in the closet, confused and paralyzed. Decisions are faster and easier now. We simply grab from our best and go.

Our initial effort created big momentum, and the process continued for about a year. We worked our way through everything and became more discriminating owners as time went on. We all picked our best things. We customized boundaries for each person. Some can successfully manage more things than others. Some can manage more but prefer not to. The kids appreciate the order just as much as the adults do.

Don't sweat this stuff. Going more minimal can be an enjoyable process. Finding funny items, retelling old stories, and reminiscing is therapeutic and often fun. We encountered things that had sentimental value, and others that once did but were no longer so important. We noticed where we had emotional attachments and made decisions that helped propel our lives forward. The interesting thing about sentimental items is that when there are fewer of them, the specific ones that you keep can be utilized more and enjoyed. These items become more significant when there is less. Instead of having ten of Grandma's things in a box under the bed to never be seen, hang one on the wall and enjoy it daily. If you encounter something that you are still mourning, determine if that is good or bad. Give yourself time to take it in or to let it go. There are a few items along the way that may take extra time. That's fine. My chosen method was to take pictures of the more personal things before hauling them off.

When I got to my books, I had to admit why I was keeping

so many. It wasn't that I lied to myself, saying that I would return to reread them one day. I didn't keep them so I could lend them to friends. I collected them because they made me feel important, smart, and accomplished. They were trophies for my ego. My desire was to no longer need trophies to validate my identity, so I let the majority of them go. Like most everything else on the tax write-off list of donations, once the items were gone, they weren't missed. Even things that initially seem painful to remove quickly become forgotten and get replaced with peace. Buying more electronic books makes the book clutter easier to manage. While we are on the subject of excess paper, go ahead and unsubscribe to those magazines you never have time to read too. When a catalog you never requested invades your mailbox, call and remove your name from the list. A reminder to covet more things and an uninvited incentive to shop for items you never needed isn't helping anybody.

With every area that we purged, more peace, calm, and joy seemed to fill the previously occupied spaces. If there was something that we came upon that we were unsure whether to keep it or let it go, we placed it in a box, out of reach. If during the year we discovered needing the item, we could retrieve it from the quarantine box. Anything that went a whole year without being missed or needed was toast. We got rid of most things after just a month or two in the box. Technically, we used our seasonal decor once per year, but we reduced that by over 50% too because it just felt so good to do it. After that purge, we started enjoying holidays much more, instead of feeling like they were such a chore.

Eventually, everyone in the house was high on the new freedom. We had more free time every day to do more of the things we loved. There was less work, more play, and more opportunities to include others. Our attitudes lifted as did our family intentions.

Playing Defense

Subtraction is only one piece of minimalism strategy. We must also think about how to prevent things from coming back. After the initial purge of my home, we settled on a purchasing system that involved mostly replacements instead of additions. We achieved a balance by refusing to allow more stuff to come in than is going out. If we purchase an item now, something else gets given away, sold, recycled, trashed, or donated. We base the main criteria for purchasing something now on its potential to create more lasting peace, instead of just temporarily satisfying the ego. Removing stressors seems to create more value than adding pleasures.

We weren't spendthrifts before, but this method has moved us to be much more discriminating consumers. It also saves a lot of money. We used the extra cash to take a few more trips each year. On those trips, we now take carry-on bags instead of checking heavy luggage. Win, win, win.

Some people pretend they are tidying up by purchasing more storage containers. Buying more bins to hide items in the basement means that we still have all the junk, plus the bins. Having a bunch of boxes full of random stuff that we will never need is not meeting the goal. Stacking boxes may provide the illusion of progress, but the point is not to move things to a new place to collect dust. We don't need to organize nearly as badly as we need to eliminate. The plan should be to move them out of your life permanently. Keep a few bins for seasonal items that you use, need, or love. Do not keep mountains of them, regardless of how neatly they are stacked and labeled. If it wasn't used or missed in a year, it probably needs to go.

Eliminate areas where messes are permissible, like the clutter closet or junk drawer in the kitchen or desk. Spaces that allow for accumulation encourage hoarding and delay decision making. Clutter attracts more clutter. Most of us have these little hiding spots scattered throughout our home and office.

Keeping these areas is like allowing resentment, anger, jealousy, or an unhealthy addiction to stick around. If the physical or emotional thing isn't helping, it's likely hurting.

Minimalism is attractive and rational when we are thinking clearly. Like so many other sensible things in this book, it's just somehow not normal. Why is the idea of having more sensible spaces and eliminating clutter so extreme? How did we arrive here? Minimalism should be standard, not radical. It shouldn't even have a name. What average people today are unconsciously doing should be labeled as "excessivism," "consumptionism," "superficialism," or at least a form of addiction. It should be commonplace to be more conscious of our physical environment. We may not have the mental faculties in place yet, but we all have a deep desire for sensible, simpler living. Advertisers know of the desire. That is why all the home improvement shows, TV commercials, and the pictures on Pinterest, social media, and in the magazines, all show minimal spaces with a few beautiful things. We are drawn to it. We desire it. But buying the simple thing in the magazine without removing ten other items does not produce the same effect. We have so much unnecessary stuff because of cultural norms, emotional instability, or unconscious habitual patterns. Maintaining a clean space for two weeks or placing a temporary moratorium on any new items may be all it takes to break the habit.

This equation must also include furniture, not just the stuff inside. Horizontal surfaces have an uncanny ability to invite more stuff. Drawers and doors can hide problems that we need to face. I had many pieces of furniture in my home that were just there because there was a space for it. We initially put it there to fill a void, not because it had a functional purpose. Why does open space make us uncomfortable? We finally admitted that several of the pieces weren't useful. So, we started moving things out and getting more comfortable with the changes. It's the physical version of what we talked about in the meditation chapter: discern, sort, and remove to allow for more open space. If you remove the bedside table that never gets used, you don't need a lamp, a picture frame, and a vase to sit on it either. You also don't need to move all those items every time you dust or vacuum. The simple act of removing one thing makes life much simpler. Do you need it? Do you love it? Do you use it? Is it life-giving? If the answer isn't "yes," then it's time to haul it away.

Taking it to the Street

After reaping the benefits indoors, I moved the mission outside. One day I was trimming the shrubs around the house, listening to an audiobook in my headphones, when I noticed just how many bushes I owned. There were three rows of decorative bushes encircling my home. Each row ascended in height, producing a beautiful, landscaped look and, I realized, a TON of work. I love mowing my grass, but I hate trimming bushes, at least when there are 65 of them. I had to do the work every few months because this particular type of plant looks terrible if not perfectly manicured. (Much like the fabric of those khaki pants that I never wore because they were always wrinkled.) I never wanted that many bushes, that's just how many came with the house when I bought it from the ardent arborist who built it. I put down the trimmer and pulled out a heavy chain. I backed my truck right up to the first bush on the front row, attached the chain, and punched the gas. The shrub ripped out of the ground and gave me a hit of dopamine. I repeated that process about five times before going back inside to fetch my wife. I gave her the keys, and she eagerly volunteered her foot to push the gas pedal while I reattached chains. We both smiled the entire time, removing 42 of the high-maintenance plants! The removal did not harm the aesthetic. We liked the new look even more than we did before.

The next week I was blowing off the driveway so that the family had a blank canvas for sidewalk chalk and a clean area for scooters and games. There was one massive tree in the yard that continually dumped pine straw and cones onto the driveway all year. It provided no useful shade, was not aesthetically pleasing, and required extra work to maintain. It wasn't even good for climbing. I set the blower down and called a professional with a chainsaw. Bye-bye, tree. I wanted to do it myself, but the last time I cut down a large tree to save a few bucks, it fell the wrong way, and I got to use the money I saved to purchase a new fence. It was a better decision to watch from a safe distance with some popcorn. The family did have fun learning how to use the rented, power stump grinder the next week, though. We enjoyed the process and permanently resolved the dirty pine straw issue. I placed more green grass in the newly vacant areas, creating more space for play, and less work.

When evaluating items that require ongoing maintenance like these, it helps to have an idea of how you want to spend your time and what that time is worth. Trading unnecessary work for more play is a no-brainer; It just requires a moment of focused attention and contemplation.

People Sweeping

The next category in my purging journey was humans. I didn't call anyone up to fire them from being a friend; I just quietly withdrew from individuals and groups that I was better off without. No one got excommunicated, just less entertained. Poor decisions involving emotional engagement with the wrong people cannibalized much of the energy I needed for the right ones. This was the case with friends, family, colleagues, customers, patients, partners, employees, and total strangers. I had many unreal expectations for myself and others. I learned how to be better at saying no to some engagements and tried to learn to say yes to better ones. More importantly, I learned to keep my mouth shut. Not only was it necessary to do in person but also behind phone calls, messages, and social media. Peacefully distancing from a select group of people was very beneficial.

This separation from people was especially necessary for me when it came to people in the news media. The media today has one job: to keep us engaged. The easiest ways to do this to invoke fear and provoke anger. Neither of those things fit into my new model for a peaceful life, so I divorced those folks too. I stopped consuming the highly biased news. At first, I was afraid that I might miss something important. I learned in time that if something significant were happening, I would find out about it. I stopped giving these propagandizing personalities my time and energy, which simultaneously created more time and energy. My attitude improved when I opted out. If hanging out with anyone, whether in person, online, or in front of the television makes you less like the person you desire to be, just purge them with the rest of the clutter.

Reclaiming Time

The final stage of cleanup involves the calendar. There are likely a few things on there that could be removed, or at least improved.

- How many things are on your schedule that offer no benefit anymore?
- How many are good things, but block the great ones?
- How many items were once useful, but no longer carry the same benefits?
- Which ones are there because of societal norms, not your values?
- What needs bumping to create an opportunity to insert the best things that are more life-giving?
- Are you living out our own insecurities through your

children's sports, academics, and activities? Are you showing up to events because of foolish desires to fit in or be seen by people who shouldn't matter so much?

- Are you purposely inserting items that shelter us from the things we need to do?
- Have some of the activities that were once fun become burdensome or started stealing joy? How many are fun but cause excessive strain on your finances or family time?

We complain all the time about how busy we are. But we must establish whether we sincerely want to change the schedule, or whether we get more benefit from ranting and fussing about it. Most of the things we gripe about are optional. They may be a social expectation of the current peer group, but they are a choice. Take an inventory. Is this the way you want to live?

Is the tee-ball coach, the dancing instructor, the golf group, the professional organization, or the civic club dictating your schedule and stifling your freedom?

Does someone else mandate when you can go on vacation, go on a date, or relax at home?

Is that permissible in your world?

Is faithfully attending 12 football games this year but never volunteering at the soup kitchen part of your plan, or did it just happen by being "normal"?

Was spending an hour scrolling on your phone intentional?

Do you want to spend your weekends relaxing and playing, or working and maintaining?

Does your calendar match your values?

Our schedules and bank statements often tell a different story than our lips. There are only 24 hours in a day and 12 months in a year. Smart people make smart decisions. Establish boundaries. Schedule wisely. Live with intention.

The Truth Might Set You Free

Having less stuff and more space creates a straightforward path to order. Let organizing be the step after aggressive purging, not a counterfeit surrogate for it. Busyness is often confused with progress. Relocation and elimination do not carry the same benefits. When we have less stuff, things naturally get more organized. A clean environment is pleasant and easy to maintain. We are less restless because there is less to do. The order begets more order. Individual progress often starts with a small task done well. Clean your room, keep it tidy, and then move on from there.

Perhaps Dostoevsky was right in his writings about the burdens of freedom, though. Maybe we are afraid of freedom because it demands responsibility. It may scare us to raise our standards and be accountable to them. Maybe being in an enclosed system where someone else makes the rules is safer and more comfortable. Do we need another authority to decide for us and dictate what we can and cannot do? Regardless, we should develop the courage to confront the relationships we have with stuff.

Aggressively defend against things that steal your time, energy, and potential. Take back control by breaking material-istic patterns formed years ago when you were less wise. Form a new identity and align it with your best self. Less stuff leads to fewer burdens. Decreased burdens lead to a more abundant life. Minimizing has the potential to induce better sleep, less stress, new opportunities, more play, extra time, and a surplus of cash. If having too much stuff produces anxiety and surren-dering some of it lessens burdens, is there any need for more discussion? Isn't it time to act?

Working all day and night for vanity is a form of bondage that only produces more suffering. To find true peace, rest, and gratitude, we must divorce vanity and allow the anxiety to leave with it. Anxiety is a call to action. It will continue to signal to us, robbing us of our potential peace until we make the changes it demands. Step up. Clean up. Grow up.

CHAPTER 12
Reworking – Work

URING THE INDUSTRIAL revolution, it was common for laborers to work sixteen-hour shifts, six days per week. Over several decades, the typical and legal workday was reduced to ten hours, then eventually to eight. In 1926, Henry ford shrunk the expected workweek for his staff from six days to five, dropping weekly work hours from forty-eight to forty. The change produced higher productivity, and many other sectors followed Ford's lead. In 1938, a law was passed stating that staff working over forty-four hours would earn overtime pay. That law as amended two years later, making the legal workweek forty hours long.

Since 1940, the world has seen incredible advances in technology, automation, education, and efficiency. These improvements have somehow not influenced the workweek to shrink, as would be expected. Only 8% of full-time workers today work less than forty hours per week. The average workweek for hourly workers is forty-seven. Salaried employees average forty-nine work hours per week. Those numbers don't even factor in the work that occurs from home or during the commute. What happened? Where did we go wrong? Why aren't work hours dropping as efficiency improves?

The (Hour) Glass Half Empty

Once again, we arrive at the same concept echoed throughout this book. Without a contrarian approach, we automatically gravitate to the middle. It's now "normal" to work forty-nine hours every week. People have agreed to this schedule simply because so many others have accepted it. So here again, we risk falling into the common trap, where average working people are exhausted, unfulfilled, and anxious. The question, for now, is not whether the culture will continue on this route, but whether you will do so. Will you make a concerted effort to claw your way out of the middle or remain there to suffer with the masses?

Before you press on, a question needs an answer. Do you desire to spend less time at work? Before giving a kneejerk response, seriously consider it. Many people say "yes" too quickly, when the answer may not be so clear. The work likely provides an escape in numerous ways. It offers a welcomed separation from many of the difficult parts of life. Some people love their work, the place where they do it, and the people involved in it. Work can function as a means to help us stay stimulated, prevent boredom, and maybe even keep us out of trouble. I don't want to assume that everyone is honestly looking to work less. Some people may have more time and a desire to give even more to their craft. But what I repeatedly hear from people around me is how there is no time left to do anything that they want to do. They're convinced that they are trapped and have no other options.

If you had four more hours free each week, how would you use it? If you doubled the time away, would you do with eight more available hours per week? Allow a few minutes to ponder that question. Let's now consider how many hours you need to accomplish your work, and whether you should manipulate that number.

In most cases, eight hours per day, five days per week

should be plenty of time to do great work. Sure, people like Elon Musk may work sixteen hours per day, but the rest of us aren't building a car company and space rockets, while simultaneously boring tunnels under busy cities. If we aren't doing those things, but still brag about our insane work schedules, we may be highlighting our handicaps, not heroism. Some people make $100K per year working twelve-hour days, seven days of the week. But someone else makes $100K working only twelve hours per week. Both may be respectable, but who is the real genius?

For the rest of the "normal" population, how much of a typical workday involves truly focused work? Most people are probably only doing it well 50% of the time. The rest is wasted time trying to enter into or return to a flow state. If you factored out all the distractions, inefficiencies, and interruptions, how many hours of work does your current job actually require? What if full immersion into the work were possible? Could you then work six hours per day and achieve the same level of productivity as what you were formerly doing in eight? Could the daily number be even less?

Some recent reports show that the average American checks her smartphone over fifty times per day. That's multiple opportunities per hour to lose flow. If it takes thirty minutes of focused work to get into a solid flow state, that means the average worker never reaches it. But it's not just the electronic notifications and texts that butt in. It's also people, environment, noise, mistakes, calls, emails, and failing systems. A polite person dropping in to deliver one quick message can quickly turn into a ten-minute chat, derailing our focus for forty minutes.

This rampant inefficiency has been ingrained into most of us early in life. Most school systems operate the same way as most workplaces. They are parallel in so many ways. It's no wonder that we perceive lackluster weeks and unnecessarily long workdays as normal. Our standards were low from early on. In our schools, we have too many levels of bureaucracy, failing systems, and inefficiencies. Too many students of differing intellect, talent, and work ethic got thrust into a one-size-fits-all model that results in the higher achievers being weighted down, shrinking back to the middle. So much of the school day is a waste.

How do so many homeschool families end their entire school day at 1:00, while the "regular school" kids go until 3:30, with two hours of additional homework each night, and a need for a tutor? Many of those homeschooled kids graduate high school a full year early and outperform the "regular school" group on the college admission exams. The homeschool probably doesn't have a teacher with multiple degrees and thirty years of experience either. How is this possible? Sure, there is something to be said for dedicated parenting, genetics, and effort, but the simple answer to this math problem is likely a combo of wasted time and inefficiency. The typical workweek is no different than the usual school day. Rampant waste, low expectations, and inadequate systems kill productivity and success.

The Experiment

Maybe you love your day job and can't get enough, but I didn't. I hated working 40 or more hours each week at the office. I despised taking any work home and adamantly defended my turf from it. If we are at work all day long, should there be homework? Get the job done and get out. Raise your standards. The work stops wherever the boundaries get set. I was intentional enough to have a moat around my house. I did not bring work tasks home. But that wasn't enough. Not only did I have other interests that I didn't have time to explore, but I was exhausted by the end of each week. I refused to spend any time on Saturday and Sunday working, but I also had no interest in spending that precious time recovering from aggressive weekly ailments. I wanted to experience more and better recreation and leisure. When I am tired, I'm a jerk. I get impatient and selfish. I don't even want to be around myself when worn out, and I'm sure my household never prefers the compromised version of me either. I was anxious and unrested, and too good to feel this bad. It was time for a change.

My businesses were vibrant and growing. I felt trapped. The machine was demanding too much fuel, and I was running low on it. I decided to challenge the 40+ hour workweek for a few months and see how it felt. The first step was simple: trim Friday's schedule. I made the adjustments to end the day at 1:00, resulting in four fewer hours per week. There was an immediate, tangible benefit to the reduction in work hours. That extra time every weekend was way more beneficial than I expected. Much like Henry Ford's experience, we did not see a drop in revenue, or to the bottom line either. The new schedule forced us to reduce waste, be more efficient, and develop better systems.

After some extended time proving that the initial cut was a favorable one, I picked up the machete again. I proposed to my staff the idea to completely eliminate one Friday per month. The reduction could only be accomplished if the team stepped up to the plate, got better at our jobs, and crammed four and a half days of work into just four. Everyone was on board, so we gave it a trial run. Everyone's attitude was better on the one week per month that we had a four-day workweek. It worked, so we doubled down and dropped two Fridays per month. In a short time, we experimented with eliminating every Friday from the work schedule. I didn't know if we could maintain traffic, revenue, and paychecks, but we had to give it a shot. After a month of four-day grinding and three-day weekends, we analyzed the results. We did it! It was a little hectic at first, but systems evolved, and competency elevated to meet the demands. We accomplished the same amount of work completed in four days that once took us five. You could look at it as a 20% increase in productivity or a 20% elimination of waste, but it was likely a combination of both. Regardless, the adjustment produced 20% more life every weekend.

Those four days are now quite busy, but the push was worth it. Everyone maintained their same pay and gained an additional full day every weekend. The workdays are more demanding but also lacking some of the emotional tension that was there before. People were recovering better on their weekends and showing up healthier on Monday. I now had the option to do work that I wanted to do on Fridays instead of only the work I had to do. The freedom was invigorating. My side projects, attitude, and playtime all began to flourish. My baseline anxiety level took yet another dramatic plunge.

The truth is that many jobs swell to the time allotted for them. I now complete the same number of procedures each week as before but have shorter time slots to do so. The changes forced us to be tighter, leaner, and smarter. We had to eliminate mistakes to survive. Our systems became more efficient because they had to. Eliminating 90 minutes of hidden inefficiency every day creates an entire day of freedom by the end of the week.

Most people's workday could be consolidated, compressed, and cut in similar ways. Modern technology allows us to work from anywhere, but also allows us to be distracted most anywhere. *Are we really working for 9 hours per day?* Of course not. Most day shifts probably involve about three hours of intensely focused work, three of moderate work, and three of distracted drivel. Could we all just go hard for five or six hours and go home? Or could we go hard for eight hours and expect a 20% raise?

My scheduling changes produced more margin, more time, and better focus. I was experiencing more leisure, play, meditation, and rest, but I still wanted to push it further. The first two work schedule adjustments had the same goal: less time working without losing any pay. The third wave required a different focus and some honest meditation. If I were to make another reduction to the schedule, there would likely also be a direct cut to my take-home pay. I had to determine what was honestly worth more to me, the time or the money. What did I truly desire more, possessions or life experiences? After all the minimizing, life no longer required the same income that it did the previous year.

I was already pondering a few things that bothered me about the so-called work-life balance that seemed to evade everyone. I certainly didn't see much balance modeled around me. As far as I could tell, most scales tipped severely in one direction. I noticed that people who made $40,000 per year, retired at roughly the same age as people that made $125,000. They had approximately the same work schedules too. The folks that made $200,000 didn't stop working any sooner than the people who made $450,000. They didn't finish the day, the workweek, or even their careers any earlier. The likely explanation for this is that people's lifestyles tend to elevate in direct parallel to their incomes. It's easy to see, but why is it so common? Is there never an arrival destination or a place of contentment? Does our culture force us to level up our lifestyle in perpetuity, never garnering any freedom or escaping the grind?

Pondering these thoughts forced me to realize that I had been keeping up with the Joneses more than I originally thought. The culture had been influencing me unconsciously, too. I wasn't competing to see who had the most luxurious watch, car, or vacations. I took pride in living beneath my means and avoiding that rat race. Being smart in this way gave me certainty and significance, even if no one else saw it. But I was comparing my business success to similar businesses around me. Even if I didn't frivolously spend the money on material things, there was still enormous pressure to produce it. I selected benchmarks and goals based on the ideas I was getting from others. After some thought, I determined that one reason I resisted cutting more hours is that I had an unspoken fear that people would see what I was doing as foolish, less legitimate, or less successful. I thrust this insecurity into the light for further inspection and found a new level of vigor for a more contrarian life. I didn't care what anyone else thought was reasonable, normal, or successful. I wanted more peace! I desired to spend more time with my family, and that meant I needed the courage to be an outlier in my profession and my community. I became okay with the idea of other people making more money than me; I just wanted to work with less stress and anxiety.

My wife and I decided that life was good enough and that we didn't need to move higher on the socioeconomic spectrum. We decided we could be content with less money, and to surrender some income for the sake of more freedom and sanity. We didn't want a vacation home or nicer cars. We wanted to experience freedom and simpler living. This plan is not for everyone, but we all need to reconsider our options regularly. If we don't define our ideal outcome, we likely end up stuck in the middle, where someone else decides for us. Our actions need to match our ideals. That may require a change in thinking, a change in strategy, or both.

I sharpened the blade and started pruning the schedule again. Snipping and slicing, I made a custom schedule that worked for my goals. It looked nothing like anyone else's work schedule that I knew. First, I gave up my lunch break. That was easy. I don't need an hour to eat. It's better to eat many small meals per day instead of one large one, anyway. If your lunch is a fun social hour, and you benefit from one, then keep it. My lunch rarely had any social or leisurely benefits. Working through the middle of the day meant that an hour could disappear on the front or back end of the day without losing any productivity. Boom, there's four more hours away from the office. I wanted more, so I started ending work two hours earlier on some days and starting 90 minutes later on others. My custom-crafted, 29-hour, workweek officially started. For the first time in my life, my focus transitioned from increasing income to manipulating the quality of life. I have not regretted it a day since.

Expanding Options

Perhaps someone else dictates your work schedule, and you don't have the luxury of making changes to it yet. But could you outperform everyone around you and ask for a more favorable schedule after proving the concept?

Could you change your work life so that there are open pockets within the typical day for doing something else you prefer to do?

Could you insert a side hustle, hobby, better relationships, or meditation within the workday once the margin is available from eliminating waste?

Should you consider another job altogether?

What would reduce your work stress, anxiety, and entrapment?

For me, it was a matter of tighter scheduling and more time off. For you, it may be a different environment, a new team, expanded roles, or delegation of some duties. The point of this chapter is not to provide a definitive, universal prescription; it's to challenge mediocrity and to push the envelope. It's to refuse to accept foolish systems that create more tension and fatigue. Your life is different than everyone else's. Your work should be too.

Where will you set your boundaries? Should people expect you to check your email every hour, or could you batch all the daily mail into one task at a specific time once per day? Your inbox is nothing but a list of demands and expectations. One person should set the guidelines for them. Should you be granted the right to work undisturbed for four hours at a time, or have you permitted people to bother you for any reason at any time? Maybe you need a "Do Not Disturb" sign or a closed-door policy for certain blocks of the day. Should non-work phone calls and texts be fielded all day long, in real-time, or could you power the phone down for your four-hour block?

Blind Ambitions

Not only should you raise our standards for how you work, you must also have a clear goal for why. Do you want to make more money in the same amount of time? Is the plan to make the same money in less time? Or are you ready to give up income to gain more free time? What will create more peace and fulfillment for you? You must decide. Otherwise, the world will force a plan on you that doesn't fit. Raise your standards. Set your custom boundaries and expectations. So many people are locked in a routine, working to the bone for someone else's dream.

Is your current job where you need to be to become the best version of yourself? Are you using your gifts and talents there? All too often, we climb the proverbial ladder for years, with all the focus on the ascent. During the climb, we unconsciously lose sight of our values and misplace parts of our identity along the way. One day, after years of toil and sacrifice, we may reach the top. From the elevated vantage point, we can finally see over the wall, maybe only to realize that we had been scaling the wrong wall the whole time. Even after that point, many will still stay there.

Many people won't leave because they have "too much invested?" They are a prisoner to the system because of factors like health insurance premiums, benefits, or tenure. The 401K match may not be as valuable as a less stressful environment, a better schedule, or an additional $15K per year at another job. The most significant benefit we could receive is the freedom to be more flexible. Is the excuse for staying in a miserable place that private health insurance would cost another $1200 per month? If so, looking for a gig that pays $15,000 more per year should be the goal so you can buy the plan you want and not be held hostage in a place you no longer need to be. But is insurance really the reason you're stuck? Or could it be the easiest excuse to delay or prevent a decision that requires more courage? When is the last time you applied for a better position?

Refining Your Focus

If your focus is growth and promotion, define the steps needed to accomplish that mission. Rewards reflect effort and competency. If you don't have what you want yet, it's most likely because you haven't developed a clearly defined desire. Or maybe you have false expectations about what it takes to get there. Do not entertain malice or envy for people ahead of you. There is no magic pill. You must be willing to suck at anything before you expect to do anything well. Work it out. Welcome the struggle and failures along the trail. They are necessary. Don't fret about setbacks. Past mistakes are bruises, not tattoos. They are also the best teachers. Learn, grow, and keep moving.

Stay in your lane and focus on specific goals. Refine the goals and distill them into small, measurable steps. A broad goal of making $20,000 more this year is usually less effective than the specific, focused goal of making $50 more during each four-hour block. The goal to work more efficiently is too open-ended, whereas a plan to put the phone in airplane mode for four hours each day is much easier to manage. Simplify as much as possible. Take one simple step and repeat it until it becomes a habit. Practice the habit until it becomes part of your identity. Measure results and celebrate your progress along the way. Children love to be measured to see how much they have grown. Adults do too. We are just unsure of what to measure. We should track several small metrics because everything we measure tends to improve. Monitor as many items as possible. No one else has to know about or understand what you are doing. There will always be naysayers. Don't internalize criticism without proper examination and meditation. Listen, reflect, and then respond if necessary.

When you see a stumbling block, remove it. If required, delete the social media apps and games off the phone. Put your television by the curb and drop your golf membership if that's what you need. Do the hard work. Small things create the difference between ordinary and extraordinary. So do them well. Sometimes more information at another seminar or planning meeting is the last thing you need; when what you really need is action—even if that action is a full stop.

It's not always about the hustle. Remember that slowing down makes us do most things better. Eating, sleeping, sex, thinking, and learning all benefit when we get our heads in the game. Don't run around aimlessly like everyone else, hoping to get lucky. Define your desires and write them down. Then make smart plans and execute them. Assess the results as you go, modifying systems, and implementing improvements. Don't delay all the gratification from your labor, either. It's essential to reward yourself for progress and discipline. Retire a little along the way by enjoying the fruits of your labor. Learn to celebrate. Gift yourself opportunities to do so.

Shaking Things Up

After trimming my main work schedule and crafting a more enjoyable lifestyle around it, I made a bold decision to take things to the next level, yet again. Since I was a teenager,

I've always had some regular job, and also maintained multiple side hustles. At any given time, I've had anywhere between two to ten sources of income. I enjoy creating new things and the game of making money. Some of those projects die, some expand, and some morph into other ventures. There has never been a shortage of ideas or desires. Even though I enjoy the side gigs, I decided to take a sabbatical for a year, distancing myself from all the additional business projects. I shut down several of those endeavors and decided not to start anything new for one year. I discontinued manufacturing, prototyping, writing, crafting, building, consulting, coaching, speaking, and designing. I politely declined many offers and stopped seeking out the others. I tenaciously worked my twenty-nine-hour main job but took a year off from all the rest.

The pullback was distressing for me in the beginning because I am terrible at slowing down and being still. I was in foreign territory. It felt unnatural and wasteful at first, but the only way to discern what I wanted and needed from life was to issue a hard stop. I needed the overall noise level to turn down, and for some of the mental churning to stop. I needed to break some patterns and do some serious contemplation. It was in that stillness that I realized how I love quiet just as much as I love the chase. For the first time in my life, I appreciated that I was more of an introvert than I had ever thought. That was an unexpected revelation. I discovered a newfound balance, understanding that some ventures were good for me, but some voids were too. It wasn't that all those supplemental ventures were terrible. They were valuable benefits to my life, but they weren't as necessary as they once were. They no longer fulfilled the same needs, and there was no reason to stay in that pattern. Those projects and experiences were teachers. I was grateful for them and for what they gave to me.

I was delighting in the extra free time, but I wanted the quality of that time to be my best too. My headspace still needed work. I could never fully relax because there were always difficult decisions to make and fires to extinguish at my dental practice. My main job was always the one that produced the most stress but was also the chief breadwinner in my income portfolio. Nonetheless, I was tired of managing, worrying, and dealing with the rigor of owning a big business. I grew to despise the many layers of management. I just wanted to do great work without so much of the drama.

So I did the unthinkable. I decided to attempt to sell my bread and butter business. With everything else stripped away during my self-imposed sabbatical, I could see that my life would be better if I could remove the burdens of ownership. I could still stay at the dental practice and work for the new owner, doing the part of my job that I was best at doing, but leaving the rest to someone else. The transition would result in a significant reduction in monthly income. But with healthy investing and minimizing, that would be workable. I wanted more peace, not more status. I wanted to be fully present when I was away from work, not fretting over all the people and processes that beckoned to me. I could live off the lower pay, owe no one anything, and put an earlier lump sum into retirement investments.

I structured a sensible proposal, and soon after, an interested buyer showed up to the table. We inked the deal. The decision made no sense to anyone else around me other than my wife, who gave me full support. Everyone else was confused and fearful. But I was resolute in my quest for a simpler life and abundant peace. I kept my custom-tailored, 29-hour schedule, but I learned what it's like to be totally mentally finished at 5:00.

The new changes produced more peace and well-being that I could have ever imagined. I did not need the prestige, power, or money to feel significant anymore. My ego began to quiet, mirroring my new environment. My mind could roam freely, which is when I do my best work. The reduction in noise and blood pressure presented a rare luxury to be more present to the best things in life.

The point of this chapter is simply to encourage you to ask some questions about your work and to consider whether your current system is an acceptable one. I am not pleading with you to take crazy risks, but rather to avoid them. What are the long-term costs of a work-life without balance, contemplation, and evolution? Life is always hard, but our work should continually progress alongside the growth of our capabilities and character. Just remember that resistance is the one thing you can always count on to show up whenever we decide to do something difficult. There is no path to peace that does not require diligent patience and fierce execution. Peace be with you on your journey.

CHAPTER 13
Cash Flow States - Money

ONEY CAN'T SOLVE all of our problems, but it can solve the money problems. And most folks have a few of those. A lack of funds can be a catalyst for severe stress and anxiety, but having money carries its share of stressors too. That principle was articulated simply by the late Notorious B.I.G.: "Mo money, mo problems." It's cliché, yes, but it's all too accurate. Money can cause a host of severe problems that never existed in the absence of it. So, if it's difficult on both sides of the money spectrum, which side is better? For someone of your caliber, a surplus is probably a preferred route. Let's go for that.

If the goal is to have security, peace, and freedom, you need sufficient funds. Saving money is a valuable skill, but it's not enough to carry you to the goal. You must also maximize your earning and investing potential. An efficient income generator, coupled with a minimalist mindset, can create a stress-reducing path to financial security. You must continue to fortify your mindset along the way and ensure that your human needs are never in desperate supply.

The initial plan is to establish a stable routine where income heavily outweighs expenses. The list of target costs includes necessary bills, healthcare, emergency funds, debt elimination, retirement investing, family needs, and a stash for recreation and leisure. The secondary plan is to use multiplication, not addition, to grow the money. I know some of you already have this stuff covered. Please forgive me if some of this material is below your financial acumen, but statistics show that the number of people lacking financial stress is minuscule. Most of us can and should make some adjustments. I can tell you from experience that slaying the money monster is worth the effort. It is an attainable goal for an over-achiever like yourself. Of course, if achieving financial stability were easy, most Americans wouldn't be in debt and under-invested.

All of us have different attitudes toward money, depending on our experiences with it and without it. Whether we idolize money or despise it, our emotional attachments to the idea of money can control us. Our sentiments concerning finance are just as important as any bank statement. Those opinions get implanted into our psyche over time by the people and environments around us. Was money ever even discussed in your home? Was it talked about nonstop? Was it always a negative experience? Where did you get your current psychology concerning cash?

Money matters are to blame for much of the epidemic of stress and anxiety people face today. Few people take true ownership and honest responsibility for them. Financial woes always rank toward the top of the list for reasons that married people get divorced and also why many others don't get married at all. It's the reason people don't move to a better neighborhood or school system for their children, and also the reason people choose not to have any kids at all. Money woes can cause grief, insomnia, depression, stomach ulcers, envy, and anger. Money doesn't create these problems, of course. It only makes them more severe. Money is a magnifier of the character and interpersonal issues that exist underneath it. With some extra dough, caring people can be more charitable. Power-hungry people can become more ego-driven. Greedy people get greedier, and insecure people raise their level of insecurity.

I'm not saying that having money or making money is wrong, just that it can be dangerous. Like so many things we desire, we too often start the chase before defining what it is we're seeking. Handing an angry kid that just left gang life a million-dollar salary to play professional sports rarely works out well. Giving volatile, lonely, misanthropic business executives a big bonus doesn't either. Fortunately, wealth rarely outpaces the growth of our character. Both take time to develop.

Let's jump into some anxiety-reducing strategies concerning money that will improve our quality of life and speed the process of achieving wealth. We'll discuss making, spending, and investing money. This methodology is by no means the only way, but it is certainly a way to achieve wealth with less anxiety and stress. The real winners in life are those who figure out how to create wealth, not just income. Wealth includes security, freedom, peace, and fulfillment.

Becoming Wealthy is Not Complicated

Ludwig Von Mises, the Austrian author of *Human Action*, wrote about economic theory through the lens of individual behaviors. He stated, "Acting man is eager to substitute a more satisfactory state of affairs for a less satisfactory. His mind imagines conditions that suit him better, and his action aims at bringing about this desired state. The incentive that impels a man to act is always some uneasiness." This seems like common sense at first glance, but it warrants further meditation. Uneasiness influences movement, no question. The thing we must reflect upon is whether our actions are helping to remedy the problems plaguing us, or whether they are just movements to distract from it. Mises goes on to lay out a model for what is required for individuals to take action. His three criteria are:

1. People must be dissatisfied with their current state
2. They must desire a different state
3. There must be a path to get there

People tend only to take action when all three of these requirements are in place. So, if you aren't moving, you should examine all three. It could be that you are not dissatisfied enough. Maybe you lack a sufficient desire for bold change. But I think most folks have little trouble satisfying the first two points, at least at the surface level. Seeing a workable path forward is the elusive part. You must define a solid strategy and an efficient vehicle to get to the destination.

On Dissatisfaction

I view dissatisfaction as a focus issue, and the path forward comes from a shift in focus. Instead of being dissatisfied with the current state, we need to think about how much more dissatisfied we will be in the absence of concrete action. What will your situation look like in one year or another decade? Who does it affect now, and who will it impact later? What other areas of life will suffer if the existing patterns continue? How much harder will the issue be to remedy when it is more severe, and we have less energy?

Pain is a great motivator. People run to drugs or other temporary fixes to dull the pain. But maybe, just maybe, the pain is there to teach us something. We should be uncomfortable sometimes. That is how we grow. Is the depression endogenous or exogenous? Is it a chemical imbalance that needs supplements, vitamins, and hormone therapy? Or, is there a crisis demanding our attention that should upset us? If I am depressed because I just got divorced, lost my job, or can no longer fit into my jeans, I'm likely not sick. It's healthy to be upset about those things because they are terrible! That pain calls attention to the fact that I need to learn something. We should use pain to achieve the leverage required to take serious action to grow. Use pain, or it will use you.

Let's look at a common, real-world example. The majority of Americans are overweight, dissatisfied with our bodies, and desire better ones. We even understand the path to get there. It's not complicated. All three elements are in place. Now what? Why can't we reach the goal? The reason we aren't moving is that we have not internalized one truth: That the pain of not doing what we need to do is far worse than the pain of doing it. In the rational world of long-term thinking, the pain of not getting into shape is much greater than the temporary discomfort of running on a treadmill. But in our emotional world, we play short term games. The thought of giving up pleasures and implementing voluntary physical agony is not appealing enough. If we stop to think about the quality of life in a decade or more, we can break a pattern of limited, short term thinking.

Do I want to be immobile when I get older?

Do I want to have multiple operations and require a box full of daily pills to stay alive?

What if the person I love most is forced to take care of me?

What will it feel like to know that my negligence caused others to give up their hopes and dreams to tend to me?

Will my condition negatively affect their relationships, alongside my own?

What about the physical pain from the compounding ailments?

Am I willing to accept the cascade of events that degrades my health and happiness?

What about the emotional pain from guilt?

What is life like when I am not able to physically play with my friends or grandchildren?

I'm not trying to be dramatic, insensitive, or rude. We

know how these things play out. We see it every day. Ignoring reality is a terrible plan, and hiding from it never works.

Let's run the same exercise for the subject of money.

What will my crushing debt load feel like down the road?

How will it affect my relationships and my health if I'm constantly stressed about money?

How many people do my financial issues affect right now?

How much worse will it be if I don't gain control?

You must have the courage to sit and contemplate all of these questions, and many more, to firmly implant criteria #1 and #2 into the deepest parts of your being. Be honest.

Are you wasting your true self by participating in "normal" activities that others are doing that are visibly destroying lives?

Where will joy and peace ultimately be found?

Is blowing borrowed money on two days of fun worth three years of indebtedness?

When we have an intense drive to get out, we can find many paths to escape. After running through hundreds of questions about what life will be if we don't take massive action, flip the table, and run through all the possibilities for what life looks like after successfully implementing smart changes. Spend some time there. How will it feel to see yourself after crushing this thing? How will you live in freedom? How will the people around you benefit from you being able to live as your true self? What awesome experiences will replace stressful or meaningless things? What will it feel like to be rich, instead of trying so hard to look like it? Visualize the future and appreciate the gravity of both sides. We need to experience intense pain, then extraordinary hope.

Income

The first topic on our money excursion is income. It's not evil to make money. Making money is not a zero-sum game. When you make it honestly, you are not snatching it from someone else. We can all win in the money game, and there are plenty of opportunities, especially for the driven over-achiever. Everyone can elevate at the same time. It's a pipe dream to expect that everyone will rise at the same rate. Equality of opportunity is possible and should be. Equality of outcome is not possible and will never be.

It's common today for lower-income earners to demonize higher-income individuals. Assuming more affluent people are shady is unfair. Assuming they were gifted their position in the absence of tumultuous work and extreme discipline is most likely incorrect. Most of us define rich people as the ones who are making more than us. For this reason, many prosperous people don't feel rich, because there is always someone richer. But if we are honest, we should admit that there are opportunities for all of us to win big, and we are already doing pretty well. Most everyone on the planet is wealthy compared to the population a century ago. If you currently make $32,500 per year, you are "the one percent" of the world. Moving on, we must recognize that it's common for the rich to look down upon the less rich, thinking that if they just worked harder and smarter, and stopped making excuses, that they could rise to the same level. This is also an unfair generalization, but social psychology shows us that people blame the victim more often than we would like to admit.

We can eliminate much of the senseless work we are doing in this comparative arena by understanding one simple truth. It's not our job to compare, sort, judge, and make predictions on everyone else's success. It's our job to do our job, regardless of the current landscape or our interpretation of it. The sooner we can stop playing these games, the sooner we can find our niche and some peace. So, what is your current job? What work should you be doing with intense focus? Whether you are a student, an entrepreneur, a salaried employee, or an hourly laborer, there is some task in front of you. We need to execute at the highest level. We must optimize our systems to maximize our performance. Before we can ask for a raise, add additional income sources, or discern whether we should find another position altogether, we must go all out to perform what is in front of us.

The process of work optimization requires some creative thinking, but mostly honesty and grit. We gripe about how hard we work, but it's all relative. We only know what we have experienced. Just because something is the hardest thing we have ever done does not mean that it's the hardest thing we could do. Something harder may arise tomorrow, and we will adapt and grow to satisfy that demand. Our limits move as soon as we encounter new territory.

Very few people work at their full potential. We are inherently lazy. We minimize efforts anywhere we can. The crux of the situation is that there are hundreds of places to sandbag on our performance. We learn early on in life where we can game the system or underperform when no one is watching. It may even be intentional so that we don't allow expectations of us to get too high. It is normal to be a slacker. It's human nature. What goes against human nature, and is, therefore, a massive competitive advantage, is the ability to maximize efforts and push ourselves to our extreme potential.

When I talk about extreme potential, I mean your unique competence. You have a specific package that no one else in the world has. That combination of skills, personality, talents, and desire is your advantage if utilized wisely. Whether you elect to use it well, and most people won't, is either your problem or your competitive edge.

Our perceived limits, which seem like facts, can be

obliterated in an instant. When life demands more of us than we thought was possible, and we pull it off, those limits suddenly change. We can wait for life to throw emergencies at us, not knowing whether we could survive, or we can train for the strength and endurance needed in those unexpected events. We have to push to determine where those limits are. It's a philosophy, a training regimen, and also an experiment. We need to test the longstanding boundaries to see how far we can go. If you have been implementing the powerful practices recommended in previous chapters, all of this will be more feasible than ever before.

Whether the goal is to add income or to add more free time, the first step in the process is the same. Maximize human potential and optimize the systems to get better work done faster, with fewer mistakes. To rework the process and design a new system for the job at hand, we may have to shut everything else down momentarily. It's a temporary productivity killer and a drain on energy to get systems in place. Nonetheless, this setback is necessary to achieve elite results down the road. It's an investment. It stinks to have to implement a new software system or learn to use new tools. But when those things save a few minutes each hour or eliminate costly errors, we begin to create more life in the margins.

The only thing we can control each day is our effort. We must decide that this will not be a place of compromise. Someone may beat us out of a position, but it should only be because they earned it by working harder or smarter than us, not because we held back. Whether you have a boss or are self-employed, we should constantly improve our positions by providing value to others. Outperform the competition, whether that is another business or the guy in the cubicle next to you. Bring your boss solutions, not problems. Provide superior value to the company. This is not just talking. We have to deliver the work to be valued as a top performer. If we have been over-delivering and going above to make money for the company and make it run smoother, then it is easier to ask for a raise. When everyone wants you for the job, you gain more clout and more options for the next promotion, which may involve another office or another career field. Opportunities manifest in the presence of great work and outstanding character. It's easy to blame our employer's lack of character when we aren't promoted, but the problem might be with our own.

When we give the work task all of our energy and focus, we can then accurately discern what step comes next. When we get better at our jobs, we find extra time in the margins that were once occupied with waste, inefficiency, and mistakes. There is fulfillment in growth, in using our full potential, and in winning. But wait, there's more. This new place is where we finally have some freedom. What do you want to do with the extra time and additional endorphins? You have options.

Do you want to use the newfound voids in the day for meditation or play? Could you add additional tasks to prove to your superiors that you deserve a promotion or pay raise? Do you desire to add an enjoyable side gig as an additional source of income?

I'll assume that there is a desire for income growth. How many ways could you grow it? You live in a fantastic time with innumerable opportunities for supplemental income. Everyone today can utilize multiple streams of income. So many people think side hustles are only for the entrepreneurial-minded. Everyone has something to offer that others will pay for. You don't have to build the next Facebook or the next Starbucks. You may not even have to develop any new skills.

The internet has created an opportunity for every person to become an entrepreneur. Years ago, starting any business required specific education, finance, legal services, risk-taking, and countless other barriers to entry. There were also many gatekeepers. Now you can start a side gig in ten minutes. If you aren't selling anything online, it may be time to do so. You don't have to build a website or form an LLC. So many user-friendly platforms already exist to make some extra dough. If you like to write, sites like Medium will pay you to do so. Perhaps you could test your skills there before writing your book. If you are good with graphic design, sites like 99 Designs will pay you to do that. Freelance sites allow you to work one task at a time in almost any field of expertise. On sites like Upwork, patrons can hire you for traditional business needs like customer service, marketing, or web development. Sites like Fiverr allow you to hire out many talents and skills. If you have a unique speaking voice, you can do voiceover work. If not, you could still be a personal assistant, a proofreader, a researcher, a transcriber, or something else. I even see people getting paid to do simple tasks that others could do after watching a two-minute tutorial video. I saw one gig someone offered to convert Word documents to PDF documents for $10. This task takes a seller 10 seconds with a few clicks. $10 isn't much, but it's easy money. Batching 20 of those in a single hour is a lucrative use of time.

Sites like eBay make it easy to sell physical products. Whether cleaning out baseball cards from the closet or finding collectibles at yard sales, many marketplaces have ready buyers on the internet. If you have specific talents for art or handmade items, you can paint, sew, crochet, weld, sculpt, build, or whatever else, and sell it on sites like Etsy. Buying bulk items overseas and selling them in smaller quantities is a viable gig if you can find a niche. Amazon makes it almost as easy to become a seller as they do to become a buyer.

Online education sites like Udemy and Coursera allow you to teach for profit. If you are an expert in something or have specific knowledge about a particular activity, you can build a course and upload it to the platform. The beautiful thing about these sort of ventures is that you build the product once, and can potentially sell it thousands of times. A published book can function in the same way. It's very satisfying to receive emails saying that more people paid me while I was simultaneously working my main job or better still, while I was fishing.

If you don't use online platforms, what else could you do on the side to generate a new source of income? So many businesses hire part-time work or temporary job-specific work. Carpentry, cleaning, delivery services, or dog walking could be options. How about becoming a speaker or lecturer at events and trade shows in your field? I did that for a few years and enjoyed the free luxury vacations and professional networking opportunities that came with it. Could you use your downtime differently? I have taken on many business consulting and life coaching clients in the evening time slots after the rest of my family is in bed. Some side gigs feel more like recreation than work. I have sold hundreds of my glass art pieces in art galleries, and glassblowing is still one of my favorite pastimes. My wife decided years ago than instead of paying to take an exercise class that she loved, she would teach it instead. She was going to do the daily cycling workout anyway. Why not get paid for it?

If you are an inventor, a creative, or a problem solver, you could hire someone from one of the sites listed above to design, prototype, or 3D print your idea. Then you could pursue licensing the product to another company or sell it yourself. I have done both. I have a 3D printer at home now. I've even licensed several products from cheap, homemade prototypes. In a licensing situation, you sign over the rights to the product, and someone else manufactures it, sells it, and distributes it. You get paid royalties and never have to touch it. Some licensing relationships can be productive for decades. The licensing route is one of my favorites because it eliminates big risks. It allows established entities to do what they do best instead of me floundering with limited resources and experience to try to make it all work. This prevents many costly mistakes and growing pains. I once received a call from the Department of Homeland Security, letting me know that a container of my products had just been seized and detained in customs. Apparently, I was missing a critical detail, that I knew nothing about, on the mandatory labels from China. That mistake came with a hefty fine and a 30-day setback.

I've enjoyed the process of product and business creation for over 20 years. The cool thing about jumping into some of these endeavors is that you become more of an opportunist. They influence you to see the world differently. One of the best ways to make extra money is to solve a common problem. There is never a shortage of problems that need solving. The solutions can be opportunities for creative people to make some extra cash. Some people get lucky. But others learn how to spot lucky situations. Making money is a skill set that takes time. Instead of trying to make a million dollars in one shot, sometimes we need to figure out how to make $100. Then to hit a million, we just have to duplicate it 10,000 times.

The next financial concept to consider is that very few people get rich or attain wealth solely by renting out their time. We need to develop passive income as well so that we can make money while on vacation, while we sleep, and while we work on other things. Passive income is how we maximize earning potential because there are only so many hours in a day. We will talk about investing for passive income at the end of the chapter, but think about long term plays that continue to generate income without requiring extra time. The goal is to be able to ride the wave and glide once finances are in order, and the pressure is off.

Spending

After maximizing income, we can shift our focus to spending habits. Many common spending practices need more scrutiny than we apply to them. For instance: If you set out to purchase a home today, the normal procedure is to find out from the bank how much you can borrow. Then that number is presented to a real estate agent who shows you a few homes at the top of that budget, if not over it. Most people buy homes based on what the bank says they can afford, not what they need, or can comfortably afford. Homebuyers usually factor in whether they can afford the amount based on monthly payments for a 30-year loan, underestimating what it will take to cover maintenance and repairs. What about automobile shopping? How crazy is it that when you go to purchase a new vehicle, no one expects you to pay for it? The norm is to get a bad deal on a trade-in, then finance 100% of the difference for the newer model for five years or more.

Modern spending behavior is far from healthy. The average American has around $5,700 in credit card debt. That's the number after averaging in all the people who don't even have a card. Of the people actively carrying a balance, they maintain about $16,000 in debt. Those are carrying sky-high interest rates of 14% or more. We make purchases similar to the people in our social circles, wondering how they are affording it. We rarely consider the fact that they probably can't afford their lifestyle either. It's all backward.

Part of getting wealthy is increasing income, but the other major component is controlling spending. People often refer to "discretionary income" or "disposable income," but they are both relative terms. I've never liked either name. All of it warrants discretion, and none of it is disposable. The problem is that we use little discernment and throw too much away.

Once again, it's time to ignore what everyone else is doing, or in this case, not doing. We have to set out a contrarian approach to spending, or we will end up in the middle with everyone else. The groundbreaking strategy is extreme, I know, but I want to propose it, anyway. It's the secret way that most every wealthy person stays wealthy. I want to challenge you to live below your means, well below your means! You get rich by earning. You go broke by spending.

Most people buy what they want, whether or not they can afford it, and defer the things that they should be doing until that fantasy day when they suddenly become rich. Not surprisingly, that windfall day never comes. We need to flip the standard system upside down. We shouldn't buy new clothes, a new car, fancy drinks, nice meals, or luxury services until we satisfy the monthly standards for getting wealthy. These things should be rewards for living a disciplined life, not a drug to distract us from the pain of not doing so. I'm not saying to give up your six-dollar latte forever. I want you to have it and enjoy, once the fundamentals are covered.

There must be a standard in place for how much of our income we will consume. Most people have no plan, so they use 100% of their income with little regard for the future. We could set a standard for what is necessary to purchase, which is very subjective. Or we can simplify the whole thing by establishing a spending number. We need a figure, so let's go with 20% for now. Let's plan to save and invest 20% of every dollar we earn. That doesn't mean we should spend the other 80%. We should put away the 20%, figure out how to live on the rest, and plan to have a surplus at the end of the year from our rational decisions. 80% is the maximum used to establish our standard of living. The ultimate goal should be much less. The great thing about the 80% rule is that you can still raise your standard of living each year. It's just that you can only do so in proportion to your rising income. The flip side of this beautiful system is that the 20% sum gets bigger as incomes rise too, pushing you to wealth even faster.

Think about it for a few minutes. How would it feel in five years to have a full year's worth of income put away? Not only is it saved, but it's invested and steadily growing. Instead of pushing right to the edge of sanity each month, you can breathe. When we are no longer sweating the financial stress of monthly bills, layoffs, or emergencies, everything seems to improve.

We should spend a minimum of 20% on ourselves the right way, by putting that money away as a gift to ourselves later. This investing transaction should be automatic. We don't need to see it, touch it, or entertain it. The money is unavailable and requires no decisions. Schedule a direct deposit every month, or every pay period, and learn to adjust lifestyle to make it happen. We must spend a few months living on 80% to learn how to modify our spending habits.

Could we rethink affordability and set the standard that we will only get a house on which we can afford to make double payments every month? A thirty-year loan that we pay double monthly payments on each month is fully paid off in less than ten years. Everyone who owns a home should budget to pay it off in fifteen years, with the goal to pay it off in even less. If we can't afford to make fifteen-year payments, maybe we should rethink how affordable it is. The interest paid on a typical thirty-year note is 250% more than what we pay in fifteen years. That means most people are surrendering hundreds of thousands of dollars to the lender in interest that could otherwise be enjoyed or invested.

Would it be so outlandish to buy a vehicle only when we can purchase it outright, with no need for financing? It might mean that we have to keep the current vehicle a bit longer or get one that isn't as luxurious on the next round, but will that crush us emotionally? Again, I'm not saying to give up the luxury forever, but to postpone the gratification until we have earned it and can truthfully afford it. The status game does not pay dividends like the smart money game. Would it be so radical to eat at cheaper restaurants, commit to eating at home, or stop drinking expensive wine and cocktails? What about the possibility of wearing clothes or carrying handbags that are missing expensive brand names? No company is paying you to be their walking billboard anyway. Brands are for livestock, to show who owns them.

What is Wealth?

What's the end goal? What does it mean to be wealthy? How do you know when you arrive there? I guess there are many answers to these questions, but my view is straight-forward. When there is enough money invested so you can live off of interest and dividends, without ever dipping back into the main principle, you have arrived. At that stage, working is optional. You can work if you want to, and do it how you want, when you want. That is serious freedom. Take a few weeks off to travel and visit friends. Work two days per week doing the thing you love to do. That sounds like a wealthy life in my book.

How to Become a Millionaire

Freedom is too vague of a goal, isn't it? You still want a hard number, don't you? Fine! Let's pick the standard, arbitrary trophy number. Do you want a plan to build one million dollars? It's a simple process. I will give you a proven model that works. You can start the process tomorrow and be almost certain that you will get there. After tackling income and wrangling spending, we can move into the discipline of automated investing.

Magic Investing

This proven model for becoming a millionaire doesn't discriminate against anyone. Everyone is on the same playing field. The way to reach a million is by building momentum using the magic of compound interest. Albert Einstein said, "Compound interest is the eighth wonder of the world. He who understands, earns it. He who doesn't, pays it." Like I

221

mentioned before, we want to maximize income through our active work, and also maximize passive earnings while we sleep. I'll give you the numbers first.

If you are 20 years old, becoming a millionaire by age 60 costs you $298 per month.

If you are 30 years old, becoming a millionaire by age 60 costs you $682 per month.

If you are 40 years old, becoming a millionaire by age 60 costs you $1687 per month.

If you are 50 years old, becoming a millionaire by age 65 costs you $2845 per month.

If you're thinking," Wait a minute. The first example only uses 214,560!" That is correct. And that is the beauty of the whole thing. Compound interest is the best friend to every rich person, and soon-to-be rich person, on the planet.

If you invest the amounts listed above, on the schedule, and average an 8% return on the investment, you hit the million-dollar mark by the target date. The S&P 500 index for the stock market (which is an index that measures the stock performance of 500 large companies in the US) has historically returned this amount, or more, over time, and required zero work from those who invested in it. At 8% interest, you double your money every nine years. Let me repeat that for clarity. With little effort, you would double your money every nine years.

If you do not take advantage of compound interest, you're crazy. I'll show you an easy way to do it. You don't even need a broker, a finance degree, or a DVD training kit from a late-night infomercial. If you want, you can send me the 3% per year that you would pay someone else to give you this same advice. By the end of this chapter, you'll know a simple, strategic process to capitalize on the phenomenon of compound interest and wealth accumulation.

Million Dollar Baby

Just in case you haven't thought of it yet, I need to shed some light on an amazing idea. If you have a newborn child, and you want to leave her a million-dollar gift one day, it only costs you $15,000. You can deposit $3,000 into their account each year for the first five years of their life, and then stop, never adding any more funds. Simply allowing that $15,000 to compound at 8% as we discussed earlier, magic happens. That little account will be worth a million at age 60.

This idea may influence your future self to have less stress and anxiety about what you leave behind in your own estate and legal will one day. You can gift the account way before your child turns 60. Hopefully, she will contribute more to the account as soon as she is able. You have options. Just know that the earlier you start, the easier it is to hit the target. It's something to think about.

A Math Game

Some people don't have to wait nine years to double their money. Many of you can do it in one day. If I met you in the street and said that I would give you two dollars if you gave me one dollar, would you give it to me? Of course, you would. You just doubled your money with zero work. What if I said that in that present moment, for every dollar you gave me, I would give two? I hope you would empty your wallet and give me every dollar you had in there. What if I went a step further and told you I would meet you back at the same spot every month to make the same trade? For every dollar you give me, up to a $300 maximum per month, I would hand you back $2. How many would you bring me? Come hell or high water, you better hustle and find some way to present me with $300 each month. You would be a fool not to capitalize fully on this opportunity every month. If it meant eating beans and rice, shopping at consignment stores, and riding a bike to work, you better make it happen. The tragedy is that this scenario exists for many working Americans, and they pass on the $3600 per year gift because of negligence.

Many employers have a retirement plan like a 401(K). The majority of those employers also offer a contribution match, meaning that they will give you an additional $1 to invest, for every $1 you contribute to your retirement plan. There is a maximum limit on how much they will match. An average match is equal to about 4.7% of your salary. So, if you make 100,000, you put $4700 into your 401K, and it becomes $9400 instantly. Listen to me. There is no better investment opportunity than this match. Nothing else offers a 100% return in one day with zero risks. Do not pass up this opportunity. But wait, there's more!

The $1 we invest doesn't only become $2. It snowballs through the magic of compound interest. For the 20-year-old, that single dollar gets doubled on the match, then invested at 8%, and at age sixty, it's worth $43. If you start at age 30, the same $1, matched and invested with an 8% return, turns into $20 at age sixty.

Maxing Out

If you don't have an employer retirement account, it's not a problem. You can set up your own Individual Retirement Account (IRA). IRA's offer some tax benefits. There are income limits for a Roth IRA, so high earning households may need to use a traditional IRA. You can learn everything you need to know about IRAs in about five minutes. Read up on the advantages, disadvantages, and limits and select one that fits your situation. Whichever one you pick, use it. Max out the contribution every year, if possible. If you want to hit a million bucks at age 60, the numbers are in front of you. We'll mention ways to invest beyond IRA limits a little later.

Simple Math & Simple Choices

You don't need a broker to tell you which mutual funds or stocks to buy. There are thousands of funds that trading managers and advisors will gladly sell you. The truth is that only about 15% of these funds return more than the S&P500 index. When you factor in all the fees, less than 5% of all mutual funds outperform the index. Fees matter because they compound too. Paying 2-3% in fees on your trades reduces your final investment dramatically. Avoid fees when possible. They may look innocuous, but they are monsters that consume your gains over time. The same $298 per month that becomes $1,000,000 in the previous example reduces the final amount to $515,000 by losing 2.5% to ongoing fees. Please tell me you saw that. A 2.5% difference in fees cost a 20-year-old half a million dollars at age 60!

I'm not bashing brokers, advisors, or the investment firms. Many people need professional help and receive solid services from those folks. Some may want to take bigger risks to try to beat the 8% that the S&P has historically returned. Other people want complex systems that produce more avenues to shelter money from taxes. You may need a sophisticated professional for your custom purposes. However, if you want a historically proven method that is easy to understand and implement, you could pick this method. Once set up, it requires no brainpower, emotion, or anxiety-ridden nights watching the stress-inducing nightly news.

I cannot give you financial advice or tell you what to buy. I can tell you what I have done to create more peace in my life when it comes to investing. I've had big gains and big losses in the past, doing hundreds of hours of research, and taking substantial risks. I've quit almost all of that and simplified the process. I now buy index funds, without a broker, that involve the tiniest fees possible. Search for the index funds with the lowest fees. Some of these may be just 0.02%. I use an online platform that is user-friendly and charges minimal transaction fees. Some do-it-yourself platforms offer $8 trades, which is nothing compared to what most firms charge. If you need more service, pay more, but do not pay someone else ten times more in fees to buy a simple index fund for you. I auto-draft money in every month and use it to purchase low-fee indexes. This method is a long term, simple play. It's also a cheap and easy way to diversify since you are buying a large mix of stocks, not individual ones. I don't look at it or fret about it. I trust the system and move on with my life.

History Repeats Itself – Don't Panic

If you take on a simple system like this and buy based on historical patterns, be patient. Don't panic! On average, there is a 10%+ correction every year in the stock market. That means a bunch of people lose a pile of money in a short time, which is why many people panic every year. We should never be surprised when it happens and should always remember as a good student of history that the market has recovered every time. It's not uncommon to see a 16% drop during a correction. The dip typically lasts less than three months before the market climbs its way back up to the previous level. Know that recessions happen, too, and will probably continue to do so. Based on history, we should expect one or two recessions each decade. They typically last less than a year. Just like the corrections, the recessions have always recovered.

Instead of seeing the market drops as horrible tragedies, smart investors see them as prime buying opportunities. We cannot time or predict the market. Attempting to do so will inevitably force you to miss some of the best gains. That's why regular, automatic monthly buying is a rational plan. Staying in the game is key. If you have surplus cash lying around and you see a 4% drop, you have the option to buy more. I make my monthly buys automatic but always try to pick up additional bonus shares on days when there is a sizable drop. I can't tell you how much better this system is for my wellbeing when compared to the models I have used in the past. I don't obsess over it anymore. I don't even get upset over market drops, because I know they are natural opportunities.

Beyond 401K & IRA

If there is extra money you want to invest that puts you over retirement account limits, go right ahead. You may need to open an additional brokerage account for this after maxing out the retirement account limits for the year. They still grow at the same rate but lack some of the tax savings that retirement accounts provide. Or you may want to invest some surplus funds into entrepreneurial endeavors, real estate, or someone else's business. I do this often, but do not use any of the cash that belongs in the nest egg. Just commit to playing long term games with long-term money before getting into riskier, more speculative ones. Do not invest in any area where you don't have adequate knowledge. Do your homework. Know that a 10% gain per year is outstanding. Be smart, not greedy. Be rational, not emotional. Trust the system. Don't worry about what everyone else is doing, including the loudmouth lying about his huge gains and hiding his regular losses.

I know what you are thinking. You want to be a millionaire at 60, but also want to be one now. I get it and fully endorse your plan. The retirement plan is just one step. Anything we do enough times becomes much easier. As we get better at maximizing income, smart spending, and steady investing for the future, we have an opportunity to live rich now. It's slow and boring in the beginning because the gains of reducing debt and increasing assets are almost invisible. Once expenses are easily covered, and the monthly retirement contribution becomes comfortable, our "disposable income," or fun money, accumulates. The long-term game doesn't abolish the short-term game.

It makes it more possible. Instead of trying to look rich, this time around, we get to feel rich. We get to enjoy vacations, luxuries, and things that genuinely make us happy without guilt. The heavy burdens from the bills are not lurking in the dark mailbox. We are more available to breathe a little and to experience true play. We begin to see the world and the people in it differently. We switch from survival mode to learning how to enjoy life and be ourselves.

Living Rich

The term "rich" means something different for everyone. Rich is a relative term based on our desires and experiences. Those things change over time. Being rich may mean eating out once per week for one person or hiring a personal chef for another. Rich may be paying cash for the fancy car for one person, and for someone else, it may be riding Uber instead of the subway. Rich could mean having the extra cash to rent a weekend cabin in the mountains for one person or owning a beach house and sharing it with friends for another. Some people want to be rich enough to work less, date more, or do more charity work. For me, being rich is not having to discuss money in my marriage. We aren't frivolous spenders, but generally, we do what we want to do without arguing or stressing about the finances. For my wife, being rich meant being able to stop working multiple jobs to stay home with our children. The ability to feed our family clean, healthy foods is another form of rich to us.

Regardless of what you classify as rich, it is important to spend some time thinking about it. Getting rich should involve living in a place of peace. What is that place for you? We not only need a vision for where we want to go, but we also need a strong enough "why" to go after it. The "why" is always about avoiding pain, seeking pleasure, and satisfying human needs. Our "why" must be compelling enough to create drive. It needs to warrant sacrifice, encourage discipline, and inspire patience. The journey will not happen without it.

The final point in this chapter is hiding in plain sight. We discussed loans and interest rates and then discussed simple investing and even more interest rates. If your credit card company charges you 16% interest, and your index funds are making you 8%, paying off the credit card is a better investment. Don't sacrifice the 401K match. But with other money, it is more prudent to attack the debts aggressively. I know this stuff is hard, but it is possible.

Gratefully, I dodged a few debt bullets in life. I've never carried a balance on a credit card. I am also fortunate to have grown up in Georgia. If you maintain a 3.0 GPA at a public college in my state, you can get an undergraduate degree for free. Incredibly, most people forfeit that massive benefit by drinking, partying, skipping classes, and screwing around. But I do know how unbelievably sweet it is to pay off grad school loans, car loans, and a home mortgage. Each of those came with more satisfaction and freedom. Realizing that I will never need any of them again is empowering. One cannot appreciate how much emotional weight is there until there is no more debt. It's worth the sacrifice.

The smart money road is one that you may have to walk alone for a while. In time, like-minded people will coalesce. Try to hang around disciplined, balanced, positive people. Attitudes are contagious. Pick the right partners in life and support each other. There should be no competition. Intelligence and integrity should be evident in the places where we work, invest, and play. If you need a mentor, trainer, or coach, seek one out. Do not be paralyzed with fear. Take courage and break down the walls in front of you. Earn aggressively, spend intelligently, and invest patiently.

CHAPTER 14
Leveling Up - Relationships

E NOW FIND ourselves in a strange place in evolutionary history, surrounded by more people than ever but still lonely. We live and work alongside so many people that never become more than strangers. Thanks to advances in technology, we are more "connected" than ever before, but a digital version of human connection is not adequate. We are starving for the real thing, but we've settled for a cheap, counterfeit version of community. We maintain fruitless relationships that serve little good and eat away at our true selves. It's no wonder that we are so stressed, depressed, and unfulfilled. Whether social, familial, or intimate, our relationships determine much of our success and well-being. If we lack healthy relationships, we cannot achieve optimal health, peace, or fulfillment.

Fortunately, when we remain deeply connected with the right people, our lives thrive. Even a single outstanding relationship can make life wonderful. Strong relationships stimulate growth, provide opportunities for play, and connect us on the deepest level through suffering. When tough times arrive, the right relationships make many events easier to endure. Allowing someone into our inner circle is therapeutic, but so is being allowed into theirs. We need people and also need to be needed.

Love is a Four-Letter Word

This chapter is about the often discussed, seldom understood, ever evading topic of love. I hope to approach the issue from an atypical vantage point that provides a framework to alleviate angst and supplement peace. By the end of this chapter, you will know exactly how to experience more love. Then you will have a decision to make.

Love is a discipline. It's not mystical or magical. It is a choice, and it takes practice to be any good at it. One does not fall into love, but rather, steps into it. Real love requires courage, discipline, and consciousness, which is why it readily escapes so many people. We cannot stand outside of love and understand it. It can only be experienced by immersion, from inside of it. Love is risky and has the potential to generate substantial pain. You know what? Let's go ahead and put it out there. It's more than the potential for pain. It's a guarantee! Pain is unavoidable if we seek this pinnacle of human inter-action, emotion, and fulfillment. There is no free lunch. Love is risky. We punish those who are closest to us, and it would be foolish to expect to be immune to that same nihilistic tendency from others. Nonetheless, Alfred Lord Tennyson's poem line still rings true, "Tis better to have loved and lost than never to have loved at all."

It is not necessary to distinguish between the many types of love in this book. Some say there are three types, and others refer to seven or more. Whether brotherly, friendly, erotic, or anything else, the formula is the same. To receive love, which is a fundamental desire, we must freely give it. This failed prereq-uisite is the primary reason so many fail to find it. To be able to love anyone, there must be an awareness that we are not alone in the world and that we are not the most important thing in the cosmos. Love is not just a realization that others are equally as important to us, but that others are more important than us. Many of us can arrive at this place with children, or possibly pets, but it's infinitely harder to get there with those who possess greater ability to hurt us.

Self-Sabotage

When we are lone individuals, only focused on and concerned with self, we always lose. Inevitably, in this isolated situation, everything gravitates toward a "me against the world" attitude. That place is where we remain permanent victims and interpret the actions of the world as personal and oppressive, even when they had nothing to do with us. Envy, anger, and depression become our only companions. We can too easily hate our neighbor for finding love and blame the world, the dating game, our career, our family, or whatever else for our own lack of results.

We all need someone to love. But it doesn't end there. If we only identify a single person to love, whether a parent, close friend, or significant other, we quickly encounter a problem. That's because it's unlikely that one person could possibly supply all of the love that another person needs. It's unfair to put that much pressure on one fallible person to exclusively deliver such an important product. When things don't go perfectly, we naturally develop an antagonistic stance between the two parties, interpreting normal tendencies and benign human behaviors as threatening acts. The worldview here is just too small. One person should not be expected to carry the gigantic load that an entire family or community should be providing.

If we can incorporate more people into the fray, some potential for healthy sustainability comes into view. We can escape the lone attitude of "me against the world" by adding a single loving relationship. But we can grow out of a dualistic mindset and sentiments of "my actions versus yours" by adding several more. When we participate in a community, there can finally be a "we" to both protect us and nourish us. A solid community of people loving each other is far more likely to pull you up than drag you down. We are collectively to blame for the lack of love. We are also the ones to take pride in the love that is being delivered. We are all in this damned thing together, and also in this beautiful thing together. No one is totally autonomous. We have all been formed by some form of community all along and continue to be.

It takes a proverbial village of some sort to live abundantly. Purposefully deciding to be a contributing member in that community increases our capacity to love. We are handicapped when we attempt to pull it off alone. Yet somehow, over time, we have lost a sense of community and togetherness. We became so selfish that we left the safety and satiety of family, whether physical or metaphysical. It seems that the better off economically we are, the more isolated we become. When we get rich, we buy more space and erect nice fences. But in times of war, poverty, illness, and suffering, people come back together. In those compromised environments, we help each other and realize how much we need one another. Then, as things improve and stabilize, we withdraw back into our private world alone.

The times I have seen the most love in my local community and family have all been just after a disaster. I've seen the true nature of people firsthand, right on the heels of a hurricane, tornado, or flood. People come together, eager to love, and ready to serve. They donate their time, money, and talents to help each other. It's a beautiful disaster. When there is a personal injury, death, or illness, I see people muster together too. It doesn't last very long, but for a brief period, I see people giving of themselves and loving each other. In those moments, people are unbelievably willing to sacrifice time and resources to help each other. We see people's best selves emerge when things are falling apart. Why is that? Why can't we stay together when things are running smoothly? Is it that we forget how much we need each other in the absence of visual reminders? Is it that we naturally become self-absorbed when people aren't dying in front of us?

Suffering seems to be the great equalizer that removes our biases. We stop competing, comparing, and judging when everyone is hurting and vulnerable. Perhaps I am overly optimistic, but I don't think we should wait for tragedy to love each other. I assume, based on the mental state and physiology we have discussed earlier, we have more energy and capacity to love at a higher level in the better times. We should not be dealing with cancer, miscarriage, or heartache alone. Nor should we stray too far from casual conversations, words of encouragement, dancing, playing games, collaborating, or community building.

Facing Reality

I contemplated a fair amount about what to say to attempt to convince you to love more freely and deeply. It's a difficult proposition, especially in the absence of propaganda, emotional manipulation, or religious doctrine. Is there a way to ask someone to give themselves away? Who would volunteer for such an experiment when the proposal guarantees the results will not be fair?

The truth is that our soul longs to give love and to receive it. We can lie about it, avoid it, or pretend it's not true, but those decisions are not long-term solutions.

We obsess over some transcendental, romantic experience of love but skirt the commitment of finding or creating it. Our success is impeded because we attach unrealistic emotions and fantasy expectations to what we assume love is. In searching for some fairy-tale version of love, we blind ourselves to reality, missing opportunities to see the real thing. We learn the ins and outs of love from people who are jaded about it themselves. This only makes us more confused and contributes to further stagnation.

But, nothing in the universe is static. Relationships are either growing or dying. Without an intentional decision to cultivate love and fortify relationships, they automatically degrade and disappear. Relationships in work, friendship, or love life wither away when we are absent. There is an effortless descent into a dark abyss when we decide to be soloists or withhold love. If our relationships are suffering, we must take some responsibility for them. If I realize that my staff doesn't love me, I must take ownership of that. I probably dropped the ball somewhere and haven't been loving them well. If my significant other wants out of the relationship, I have likely failed to give of myself to meet her needs. Honest awareness should prompt some action, but what comes next?

Before having any chance to love others well, we must first love ourselves. This sounds cliché, but it's true. Love is about sacrifice and service. It's almost impossible to offer our love when we are wounded, tired, or compromised. The point of loving ourselves is so that we can then give our best to others. If we cannot find something outside of ourselves that warrants our love, we will fail. We won't be able to give an adequate supply and will not receive much either. Selfishness is the major impediment to love.

Please hear what I am saying. When we attempt to love ourselves, it must still be about someone else. Never establishing the right focus is the reason so many fail at self-love. Self-pity and anger are neither love of self nor of others. They're just selfish. So, in order to love yourself, identify who else will be a recipient of it. Think about it and carefully select someone to work for. Who do you love? Who do you want to love? The key person might be someone you have not met yet. Maybe you decide to love yourself so that your future spouse, children, or community will be able to receive your best. Regardless, the point is to build the capacity to become a better lover, so that you can make people's lives better. This, in turn, contributes back to your own fulfillment. It's a long-term compounding effect, just like retirement investing. Love doesn't just change what you do and what you have; it changes who you are.

What's Your Love Level?

Before we get into the practical steps for becoming a love machine, let's take a bird's eye view for some quick evaluation. These levels apply to all relationships, whether familial, communal, or spousal.

Love Level 1

Many of us end up in an elementary form of love, where we only participate if it benefits us. We take more than we give in level one and have no remorse about it. Some could rightfully argue that this is not loving at all, only a form of connection. When in a level one relationship, we may be somewhat open emotionally, but only as long as there is a guaranteed benefit for me. It's all about me and what I want. People who live in this stage often believe that everyone else is greedy, self-seeking, and untrustworthy, just like them. If we do things for other people, it's only with the expectation of self-gratification. These behaviors are probably not discussed with the other party. We just assume what's coming to us. Many people never make it out of this level. There is no authentic connection here, no sense of "we," and certainly no intimacy. Level one is about taking. This type often results from hurt, fear, immaturity, or plain old selfishness. There must be some internal healing before leaving this level. These relationships never get off the ground and are lost in the blink of an eye.

Love Level 2

A level two relationship is more of a mutual agreement, still maintaining some focus on self-desires. This is a contractual relationship in which I will give you what you want, but only if you give me what I want. If either party fails to fulfill the terms of the contract, the deal is off. We are still self-serving at level two but agree to a less hedonistic, somewhat cooperative relationship. As long as each party is getting what they want, things move along. However, since both people are constantly keeping score and monitoring the other's behaviors, they are ready to withdraw their end of the agreement as soon as there is a breach. If you don't include me in your friend group, you cannot borrow my car. If you don't stop riding my case about how much money I spend on clothes, I won't give you sex. If you won't feed my cat while I'm out of town, don't ask me to check your mail while you are away. If you allow me to watch the big game on Saturday, I will patiently listen to you talk about your issues on Sunday. I will cook your supper and do your laundry until you fail to acknowledge me for it. We are just bartering and negotiating in level two, not freely giving without an expected return. It's always a bargaining relationship. Some people call this horse-trading. Others call it whoring. You can stay friends and even stay married at this level, but there is little intimacy.

Love Level 3

A level three relationship is one in which the focus is totally on the other person. There is no scorekeeping. Fairness is not even in the equation, because we feel the other person deserves to be loved more, even if they aren't the best at giving it. There is a level of sacrifice and giving at level three that presents as a one-way gift, not a trade. We can love people in this way as friends, family members, colleagues, or lovers. There is a profound sense of humility needed to deny the self and serve someone else in this way. These decisions produce deeper connection and adoration, increase intimacy, and create security. Hopefully, both parties learn how to love at this level. But even if there is no reciprocation, love is still offered by the committed giver. Gratitude plays a big part in being able to love at level three. When we are grateful and feel like we have more than we need or more than we deserve, we are more capable of being a generous giver. On the other hand, it is impossible to be grateful when we feel entitled. Level three requires emotional stability. For those who have become proficient at this level of loving, they recognize that behaving this way satisfies their own human needs too. When we freely give our time, money, or attention, we get some significance, connection, variety, contribution, growth, and certainty.

Level one is about taking. Level two is concerned with trading. Level three is focused on giving. But there is still one more level.

Love Level 4

Level four love would seem unattainable if not for some special people in the world that have demonstrated that it is possible. Few accomplish it. Those are the Mother Teresa and Nelson Mandela types. In a level four love, we not only love those closest to us in a manner mimicking level three, but we begin to love everyone this way. At the highest level, we are willing to love friends, family, strangers, and even our enemies. Everyone is considered equally deserving of love and equally flawed as humans. Level four love requires us to identify deeply with all human suffering, to give people the benefit of the doubt, and to assume that how we treat them matters significantly. In this mindset and worldview, we can see all people as brothers and sisters, as needy and broken members of the community. A higher capacity for forgiveness and a minuscule level of judgment coexist. This type of love is a conscious decision like the others, but level three and four require a different mindset and identity. Love must be a state of being at the higher two levels, becoming a part of our being.

A Simpler Directive

Why did I include all of this relationship stuff in a book about stress and anxiety? Because once we decide that love will be our mission, life becomes simpler. We don't have to exhaust ourselves deliberating over fairness, comebacks, revenge, or self-preservation. There are fewer contingencies involved with deciding how to act. The choice is simple. That is to love. The mission is difficult but does not waver. We cannot appreciate the freeing nature of these concepts until we live them out. They eliminate so many countless hours pondering decisions and responses. When we choose to be love, we minimize the clutter and escape wandering emotions. Simplicity creates more peace with much less energy.

We usually live life forward, but often understand it backward. Maybe it's time to be proactively preventive, allowing the best things to grow stronger and require less repair. If we do intend to raise our loving to the next level, what does that look like? This stuff sounds deep and complicated, if not downright impossible. What specifically are we supposed to do from here?

You will have to discern the right strategies based on each relationship. But from a practical standpoint, it does not have to be complicated. We simply have to show up and to give. There are ample opportunities every day. For example, after a long day at work, instead of grumbling and complaining about it, give your spouse that massage that you desire. Yep, take your sore back and offer her your time, energy, and attention. Make the rest of the day all about her. If you have three missed calls from a long-winded family member that you don't want to talk to, pick up the phone, and freely give them twenty minutes of your time. If your friend is mourning from a tragedy, don't text, "Let me know if I can do anything." Instead, do something. Deliver dinner and sit with him. Give him your time. Be present. Actions speak louder than words, to both parties. If your coworkers are stealing your food out of the break room, take in a huge basket of food as a gift for the entire staff. Put your phone on airplane mode, turn off the TV, and go play a game with your kids. Pass up the golf tournament this weekend and volunteer at the soup kitchen or visit a shut-in. The action doesn't have to be awkward or uncomfortable. It just needs to be unselfish. Just act in a way that benefits someone else. This is an unbelievably powerful tactic to break undesirable patterns and mend relationships.

In the beginning, these actions are a matter of discipline. The initial progress is in denying normal guilty pleasures and selfishness. But over time, as we spend more time close to people and relate with them, it doesn't feel so much like work. As we see the humanity of others, we appreciate their suffering. We become less judgmental, more forgiving, more grateful, and less triggered. We develop compassion for others and a passion for serving. When we appreciate that our love matters, we want to use it more.

Q and A

Moving on, it's time for a few questions:

- Within these four levels, where do you spend the majority of your time?
- What types of relationships exist in your life?
- Who do you keep at level one?
- Is level one fair, sustainable, or even worth maintaining?

- Should that relationship grow into a level two or three, or be dissolved?
- How many people do you cooperate and trade within level two?
- What are the negotiating tools and tactics?
- Are you a codependent hostage or a hijacker?
- Are those relationships stagnant or decaying?
- Do you want more out of these relationships?
- Who have you kicked out of this level because of broken contracts?
- Who needs pardoning, forgiving, or another chance?
- Who should receive level three love from you?
- How would the people you love most respond to love at level three?
- Are you willing to go first?
- Are you willing to keep up the practice?
- Do you think that level four is possible?
- Do you desire the peace that would come from this mode of existence?
- Are you willing to surrender anger, jealousy, pain, judgment, and other barriers?

Don't rush these questions, especially if they are uncomfortable. Write down long-form answers to each. Get into a powerful and loving state, and ruminate on the individual people and your history with them. Consider that what you remember may not even be true anymore. If we want high-level relationships, we must have elite discipline and elevated thinking. That starts with integrity and humility. In pondering our human connections, we are forced to see when we were selfish, unfair, or reacting out of pain. It is then that we can develop a plan for improvements. Know too that these realizations only happen when we are well-rested and open to truth.

Loving Discomfort

When I started spending purposeful time on these issues, I had many hard decisions to make. I started to see things I had never seen before. I knew that I had run over and hurt so many people because of brokenness, selfishness, weakness, and ignorance. I knew I needed to apologize and hope for some reconciliation with many of them. I also knew that I needed to elevate my love or to separate from people that I was using and mistreating, for their sake. The reparations were not immediate, and some of them were declined. Nonetheless, I had to start the process of learning to love better.

As I attempted to learn how to repent, repair, and reinforce, I started asking myself uncomfortable questions about specific relationships. This was a painfully enlightening process. After something went sideways and there was drama, discomfort, or disarray with someone, I developed a new discipline. I would sit alone and ask what I had done to make these unfortunate events occur. My old way was to focus on all the things the other party did wrong, and on what was wrong with that person's character. The new model put me front and center. Blaming others was not an option. I would sit alone and ask myself, "What did I do to contribute to this mess or make it worse?" That's a hard question, but one that generates answers.

I decided to start loving specific people at a higher level. Some of these people simply received better treatment from me without any advanced notice. Others received phone call confessions, emails, or letters of apology. I decided that I wanted to be less wounded, more merciful, and show greater compassion. To love better involved seeing other people's pain, as well as my own. I elected to take more responsibility for my actions and appreciate the gravity of my selfish decisions. This meant I had to stop blaming others because I was a large part of the problem. What people do is usually not what they are. Often, what they do is what was done to them. It's a crazy phenomenon that we will pass on the very things done to us that we hated most. Everyone is operating from a wounded state. We must remember that. All people are suffering.

I was once forced against my will to discover an impactful practice for seeing other people in a new light. On a remote wilderness excursion, my guide dropped me off at daybreak in the middle of nowhere. The original plan was for him to pick me up at a rendezvous point a few hours later. But a setback occurred, and plans changed. He let me know that he would not be back until after dark. I didn't have a plan for how to use the remaining nine hours of the day, so I devised one. I decided just to let my mind roam, to enjoy having nothing to do, and to be one with nature. That plan bombed miserably after about 52 minutes. I became bored. I still had a long way to go, so I came up with an unorthodox plan C. I decided to select one personal relationship that needed work and to focus on that person for a full hour. I started meditating on and praying for that specific person. My consciousness and my prayers expanded as the hour passed. I prayed for specific pains, experiences, and tragedies that the other person may have encountered in life. I could infer what some of those may be. I started seeing the person in a different light, as a fallible human and a wounded child. I became more sympathetic and more compassionate. I started to understand and to forgive. This impromptu therapy session was intensely emotional and changed relationships permanently. I repeated this process for eight different people that were important to me. I was exhausted by the end of the day. Eventually, I saw headlights piercing through the darkness coming to retrieve me. It was a start metaphor for what was also happening within my soul. The darkness was dissipating as light emerged. This exercise is extreme, but some version of it may be useful for you too.

I cannot begin to explain the amount of peace that filtered my life when I proactively started trying to level up my love.

I wasn't a monster before. Most people would have probably classified me as a pretty good fellow. But I wanted to live in a different state, whether anyone else understood it or not. I wanted freedom and peace and believed that love was the prerequisite for it. That meant I needed to control more of my actions and surrender more of the outcomes. When I began to invest in loving at higher levels, which is difficult and risky, the dividends were evident. This was the case even if there was no response from the other party. It doesn't require outside recognition or appreciation. The satisfaction is internal, which makes it much harder to lose or to have stolen. Love is becoming more a part of my identity.

Staying the Course

The lighthouse that we are sailing toward is love. We will be battered around by storms, and probably get sick at points along the way. But if we set our coordinates properly, we can get soaked, battered, or sick without losing our minds and jumping off the boat. We must be careful because it's an emotional process.

Emotions are not all bad. I am not saying that we should deny emotions, just that we should consider which ones are necessary and useful to keep around. We should recognize the emotions, and ask why they are there, but they should not control us. People will say, "Follow your passion." But passion is dangerous. "Follow your prudence" may be a better slogan. People also say, "Trust your gut." But there should be a caveat to that one too because most guts aren't in the best health and have not been trained enough to be trusted. Be present to the emotions, take them seriously. They are very diagnostic and will show us what needs work. Emotions should motivate us to be better, not cripple us. Use them to learn and grow, becoming less reactive all the while. It's permissible to be angry, but not okay to do it unconsciously. Sit with the anger. Diagnose it and make a plan.

Often, the most loving thing we can do is not preferred by the other party. Being liked is not a prerequisite to giving love. Having an ideal, enthusiastic recipient is not either. The people who need it most are likely the hardest to love. Remember that conflict, fighting, anger, and selfishness may be meeting needs for other people. Some may not share your desire for peace. Their patterns and addictions do not change your strategy.

Committing to love better may mean casually leaving many of the circles that gave us some identity before. Some groups live under the guise of virtue, fairness, and liberation, but can lead us into bitterness and tribal warfare. Maybe it's better if we don't clearly identify with any one group or fit into one box. What if we got to a place where we sincerely wanted to get to know people, without being threatened by the differences. Until we surrender our fear and anger, we cannot see the wounded child inside of others. Some people still have small hearts and minds. The question is whether they should be condemned for it, or loved out of it? The secondary question is, who should be offering the love?

The process takes time before people will settle down and lower their guard. We don't expect a traumatized, formerly abused, adopted pet to relax on day one. But we do trust that, over time, we can love them out of their fears. It's probably expected that we will get bitten a time or two, and we understand why. The process for people is the same. Healing, safety, and adoration create a willingness to be more honest, more vulnerable, and more generous. Hopefully, those things reciprocate. Whenever we receive a gift we didn't deserve, we often feel a call to give more too. It's human nature to share in times of abundance. In time, maybe we can learn to share even in scarcity, which is even more powerful. When we voluntarily offer the best of ourselves, intimacy grows. The other party feels more loved, which makes them more secure.

In this process, don't forget your tongue. Practice responding after contemplation, rather than instant reaction. Be precise in your speech. Use honorable language, not reckless emotions. Offer praise without solicitation, but no critiques without invitation. Pay compliments and make them sincere and specific. Language and tone are vitally important. Disrespect is for losers, not lovers. Do not verbally jab, cut, or demean someone you love in front of others. Saying things in public that we don't possess the courage to say in private indicates immaturity and cowardice. Never threaten the people you love, ever! Threats concerning withholding love cause permanent damage. Give people the freedom to express themselves without an attack.

This love stuff is difficult but possible. When a few people are successfully doing it, but the majority cannot pull it off, there can only be a few explanations. It is either not taught adequately, not modeled well, or just plain difficult. I think all three apply. Real love is not an intuitive process. It won't happen by accident.

The path to love is more circular than linear, but the progression is something like this: In order to receive love, we must freely give it. We must love ourselves first to raise our potential to love. The way to love people more deeply is to be in a position to see their suffering.

The catch is that we can only see their suffering when we move away from the mirror and get closer to them, physically and emotionally. If we have not ourselves suffered sufficiently, our vision is handicapped or not yet developed. If we have not experienced suffering yet, it's even more important to enter a community, because ours is coming. We will need help too. Within a community, we can begin to live in a state of love, sharing our bests with one another.

Maybe at the core, even our desires to love are selfish. If that is the case, use your selfishness, or it will use you.

Our capacity to give and to receive love seems directly proportional to how much we purge the self. In cleaning up our baggage, we make room for something better. It is the dying process that produces new life. We cannot hold on to the old way. If we can let go of the tired, broken, empty, loneliness, we can welcome the new season of growth. This process protects us because if we are no longer focused on the self, we cannot be hurt as badly. Real love should not have qualifiers and conditions. Loving people freely means doing so without a hidden agenda. It's the only way to move towards the top tier. External validations are nice, but no longer required for us to feel accomplished. It's not a bad thing if we feel special, but it is insidious to take a position that others are not.

When we move into a higher level of loving, we no longer have to be shocked and dismayed that others are operating in the typical framework. Most individuals have never seen it modeled well. That is a reality, but it does not affect your mission of love. Productive action with a deeper understanding of human needs is gratifying. Soulful people spread peace and inspire more of it. They do not engage in futile, selfish endeavors. They are happy seeing others progress and delighted to contribute. Great people come to serve, not to be served. When the normal default is selfishness, people notice when they see selflessness. It's noteworthy and undeniably attractive.

It's easy to say that I will die for someone. It's much harder to live for them. Most people give it a half-hearted try and give up, not appreciating that this is a marathon. The masters are patient and intentional. Prepare. Show up. Do the hard work. Level up.

Whether you are religious or not, consider the brilliant words of Francis of Assisi, a man known for his level four love of people, animals, and the earth:

Lord, make me an instrument of your peace:
where there is hatred, let me sow love;
where there is injury, pardon;
where there is doubt, faith;
where there is despair, hope;
where there is darkness, light;
where there is sadness, joy.
O divine Master, grant that I may not so much seek
to be consoled as to console,
to be understood as to understand,
to be loved as to love.
For it is in giving that we receive,
it is in pardoning that we are pardoned,
and it is in dying that we are born to eternal life.
Amen.

Outro

WHEN YOU INITIALLY picked up this book, you did so with a healthy curiosity and some expectation for change. I assume that you've experienced considerable traction in a positive direction since that day. I hope that you received substantially more than you expected. I suspect that your desires and expectations have grown alongside your habits. The book is now coming to a close, and you have some decisions to make.

I hope you've been provoked and challenged by my persistent, introspective questions. My goal was to provide as many questions as answers and to inspire you to revisit them often. It's now time to consider where you need to go from here. With that in mind, I have one final question to ask:

Who do you want to be?

The answer to that question determines what comes next, and what intensity you need to bring with you. There is only one person who can answer the question and only one person with the agency to bring it to fruition. I know that if you made it this far, you possess a valuable gift. That uncommon package is a combination of creative vision, character, and an appetite for growth. You don't belong in the middle. You know this and have always known it. It's time to permanently opt-out of common mindsets, behaviors, and relationships, and live the life you were designed to live.

Character does not change from mere discussion. It develops through contemplative action. We are what we do, not what we say. It's no longer acceptable to wander unconsciously, participating in foolish games that prolong unnecessary turmoil and fail to produce lasting benefits. You must continue to behave in a manner worthy of your true identity. That identity is a product of what thoughts and actions you are willing to repeat.

You may have to go it alone for a while, forfeiting the shelter of mediocre environments that no longer measure up. It's time to cleave from a loose, collective identity and to establish a secure, individual character. The accountability there is not for the faint of heart or for those who prefer excuses. As Carl Jung put it, "Collective identities are crutches for the lame, shields for the timid, beds for the lazy, and nurseries for the irresponsible." For an honest over-achiever, there is only one path forward. Solidify your target and go. There is plenty of work to be done. Fortunately, your best self will continue to signal to your current self, presenting reminders and offering opportunities to prevent complacency. Don't ignore those messages. You have an undeniable calling to something greater. Don't hide from it. Take courage and answer the call.

You're too good to feel this bad.

Made in the USA
Monee, IL
14 October 2021

80045566R00152